OH SNAP!
MY CAREER IS IN CRISIS

Advance Praise

Great book and great writing style.

I found myself in the waiting room with Gladys Kravitz and the other patients at the Career Crisis Clinic. You will most likely identify with one of Maggie's characters you meet in the doctor's waiting room early on, or perhaps you suffer from some symptoms of one or more characters. Treating your career crisis like a Doctor treats a patient, allowed me to really connect with the process and the treatments (recommended actions). Maggie intersperses humor throughout and I honestly felt myself relaxing, it was going to be OK. As if all of that is not enough, her work is based on real clients and real situations. She not only wants her patients (take that as readers) to get out of the crisis but to thrive and be happy.

Ok so I thought, great another self-help book, so I dove in with an expectation of just having common sense restated, and I was quickly disappointed. Maggie writes like someone who has lived and survived in the corporate jungle and came out with wisdom and a flair for keeping me engaged through the whole journey. She does a masterful job of bouncing between corporate wisdom and career advice. It does not matter which of the career crisis's you are suffering from, her advice will help you find clarity and develop a strategy to put a plan in place. So do the exercises and learn what's holding you back and where you want to go, and most of all how to get there.

— Dr. Michael R. Spano

I've worked as a project manager for 20 years and I've attempted to create "project plans" for my life and career path in the past, but they never really worked. Turns out I was missing a Strategy, my guiding star! Thank you, Maggie, not only for the idea but for the step-by-step guidance on how to go about it. Brilliant!

— Suzanne Manker, Project Manager

Never Too Young

Although I am a young adult, and I am just starting my career, I found this book to be full of advice that currently applies to my life. It is easy to get caught up in the stress of trying to get ahead in one's career, constantly moving from one stage immediately to the next, that one forgets to pay attention to all the other important facets of life. This book made me realize that you are never too young to question the path you are on, and it is important to check in with yourself and make sure you are on a path to a well-balanced life! Her book helped me to properly plan out what I want from my career so that I did not make any rash decisions or suffer from "analysis paralysis." I would highly recommend this book to other young adults who, even though they are just starting their career, want to make sure they are on a path to a career that will complement their lifestyle.

— **Madison E.**, Graduate Student

When Maggie talks, people listen. That's because when Maggie talks, she tells it straight up, and you know she knows what she's talking about! So in this, her third book, you will find a trustworthy guide for meeting your own career crisis with courage, curiosity, and clarity. With detailed, step-by-step guidance, lots of examples, and a comprehensive workbook, "Oh Snap!" delivers everything you'll need to develop an actionable, living strategy—everything, that is, except the commitment I predict you'll want to make to follow the book's brilliant lead. Here, "strategy" becomes more than just a linear, tactically driven plan. Following the guidance in this book, you'll create a dimensional, soul-inspired way to craft the work you're meant to be doing, in alignment with your core vision and values.

— **Kimberlie Chenoweth**, Author, Mentor, and Founder of
The Wholeness Project™ www.thewholenessproject.com

I just love the way Maggie Huffman writes! Even the credits and biography were a pleasure to read. The whole time I was reading this book I knew I was being coached, but it felt so comfortable. I knew the exercises would be work, but I was invited into them with such an amiable sense of humor that I was undaunted. I might actually approach my career—and my life—with a real sense of purpose again. Thanks for reminding me!

— **Ruth E. Wells**

I just finished reading *Oh Snap! My Career is in Crisis*, because I was curious about the title. Although I'm not currently in a career crisis, I have definitely had crises in the past. What I found the most helpful in reading this book is that it's not just a way to confront a crisis in your career but also helpful in navigating life's changes. I found the author's method to be simple, elegant and effective. As a career counselor, I'm going to give this to many of my clients as a practical tool.

— **Shirley Clauss**, Career Counselor

I loved this book! In "Oh Snap!" she has again drawn from her own life experiences to provide tools to inspire us to rekindle the light that we were all born with to guide us toward our best selves. This not only is invaluable in making career choices, but in all aspects of our lives. She has done this with no judgements, no pressure, no preachy lecturing, but with loving encouragement, and the rousing enthusiasm of a cheerleader. Realizing that the journey from fear of the unknown and self deprecation to achieving empowerment requires curiosity, courage and lots of work, the author lays out a plan to help remove those stumbling blocks, sending us down the path we've blazed for ourselves to discover what floats my boat, makes me happy, makes a difference!

It's not just the Army that helps you "be all that you can be!"

— **Marcia Sheaves**

Oh Snap! My Career is in Crisis is for everyone who wants career/life balance, and fulfillment from the life they live. From a professional home manager to a C.E.O. of a prestigious corporation this is a book that will transform your life, beginning with where you are now. As a scrapbooker, the process of crafting my career or life purpose really resonates with me. The R.I.C.E. perspective allowed me to relax about the process of examining my job history and the artful approach of the workbook made it fun and exciting to explore new career possibilities. I also found myself doing the guided visualization from chapter 7 on a run, proving that her "work-outs" are user friendly! I was inspired to create a new life/work strategy where I could volunteer in combination with a job to craft my next career. Truly Transformational!

— **Katherine E.**

A crystal clear approach for achieving the most out of our life expectations. In her uniquely comfortable and humorous style, the author specifically targets a method of achieving maximum career satisfaction.

The engaging narrative offers an excellent map for designing a personal strategy tailored to suit each individual. Each chapter asks creative thought provoking questions, followed by a practical method of utilizing thoughts and desires into an achievable and practical personal plan. The workbook portion of the book is a vital instrument in developing the comprehensive big picture. Maggie has produced another winner, for sure!

— **Marie Ottoboni**

I was pleasantly surprised to find *Oh Snap! My Career is in Crisis!* went way beyond theory. It skillfully leads the reader through a process that expands and clarifies your understanding about what you want and need with regard to a career. I found the workbook and exercises, to be very effective tools, which helped me to develop a real clear career strategy and an effective process to get there! Whether you are a young person, searching for what you want to do with your life, or someone who needs to make a career change, I recommend this book.

— Christine Matthies

Maggie does a great job drilling down into what are the key needle-movers to build a career - but not just any career; a career that creates the life that you want. She gives the solution to moving from crisis mode to fulfillment mode.

— Mel H. Abraham, CPA, CVA, ABV, ASA,
Author #1 Bestseller, *The Entrepreneur's Solution*

OH SNAP!

MY CAREER IS IN CRISIS

Craft a Strategy to Get Your Career Back on Track

MAGGIE HUFFMAN

NEW YORK

NASHVILLE • MELBOURNE • VANCOUVER

OH SNAP! MY CAREER IS IN CRISIS
Craft a Strategy to Get Your Career Back on Track

Published in New York, New York, by Morgan James Publishing in partnership with Difference Press. Morgan James and The Entrepreneurial Publisher are trademarks of Morgan James, LLC. www.MorganJamesPublishing.com

The Morgan James Speakers Group can bring authors to your live event. For more information or to book an event visit The Morgan James Speakers Group at www.TheMorganJamesSpeakersGroup.com.

Shelfie

A **free** eBook edition is available with the purchase of this print book.

CLEARLY PRINT YOUR NAME ABOVE IN UPPER CASE

Instructions to claim your free eBook edition:
1. Download the Shelfie app for Android or iOS
2. Write your name in **UPPER CASE** above
3. Use the Shelfie app to submit a photo
4. Download your eBook to any device

ISBN 978-1-68350-343-9 paperback
ISBN 978-1-68350-344-6 eBook
ISBN 978-1-68350-345-3 hardcover
Library of Congress Control Number:
2016918664

Cover Design by:
Rachel Lopez
www.r2cdesign.com

Interior Design by:
Bonnie Bushman
The Whole Caboodle Graphic Design

Editing:
Cynthia Kane

Author's photo courtesy of:
Beryl Young

In an effort to support local communities, raise awareness and funds, Morgan James Publishing donates a percentage of all book sales for the life of each book to Habitat for Humanity Peninsula and Greater Williamsburg.

Get involved today! Visit
www.MorganJamesBuilds.com

DEDICATION

• • • • • • • • • • • •

I dedicate this book to all of the people I have ever
worked with in my life—for money, fun or music!

TABLE OF CONTENTS

• • • • • • • • • • • • • • • • • • • •

ARE YOU IN A CAREER CRISIS?

· ·

"Always remember that you are absolutely unique.
Just like everyone else."
—Margaret Mead

Hello!!! Welcome to the Career Crisis Clinic. The doctor (we use that term loosely) will be with you shortly. Could you please take a seat? There are a few things for you to read on that table over there.

So you take a seat on the uncomfortable orange plastic chair. You sneak a look around at some of the other people sharing the waiting room with you. There sure are a lot of them. You hope you don't have to wait very long, because you are really in a bad way, and these chairs are *very* uncomfortable. They're supposed to be molded, but to what? They certainly don't fit the shape of your butt—er, excuse me, seat. And that muzak! It doesn't help at all. The other people look pretty miserable, too. Even though you don't see any blood or broken bones sticking out, you still get the feeling that there are some serious emergencies here.

"Why are you even here?" you ask yourself. Oh yeah, that's right—you've done a little bit of self-diagnosis, you're pretty sure that you're in a career crisis, and you want to find out about your options.

"Wow, there are a lot of people here. Does everybody here have a career crisis?" You lean over and mention this to the complete stranger sitting next to you.

"Oh yeah. This is career crisis city. I've been here lots of times, so I can give you the lay of the land." She eagerly jumps into conversation. If you ever saw the old Bewitched TV show, then you'll recognize her immediately as the first Gladys Kravitz, which works out well because she really knows the scoop. "Let me tell you about some of these folks. Maybe you have the same thing going on."

"See the woman over in the corner on her iPad? She's answering email. She'll get a phone call from work in…oh there it is, right on schedule. That's Lisa. She can't sit still for a minute, and they're always calling her for one thing or another. See how tired she looks? And stressed? And she didn't have lunch today. She's not sleeping too well either. She's here because she's had a couple of stress related health scares, but she still can't stop working. She's in a work/life balance crisis, and she just can't see how to get out of it. Her job demands so much from her."

"And next to her is Mitch. He had a job for 22 years in the financial district downtown. The company moved to the Midwest somewhere, and he didn't want to move. So he took a package. Now he wants to find a new job. But he doesn't want to do the same thing. He realized that he accidentally got that job, and accidentally stayed there all this time. He didn't really make a decision, it just kinda happened. He feels like he was numb before, and he just woke up. Now he has no idea what he wants to do next. He just knows that he wants to make a decision about it this time, not "default back to numb."

"Next to him is Lori. She has horrible migraines. She's had them for years. She's pretty sure they're related to stress. She made the connection that she's had horrible jobs for years, and she's had migraines for years. She wants to make a change, but she doesn't know what she could possibly do with these debilitating migraines. And even if they are stress related, will they recede if the stress is lowered? And what does she want to do? She doesn't know."

"Tyna, next to her, has been burned by some pretty bad work situations, too. She actually does know that she wants to make a move, but she's pretty risk averse right now, as you can imagine. So she feels frustrated and trapped. She wonders if she is too afraid to make the move that she knows she *wants* to make."

"That woman in running gear over there? That's Louisa. She took time off in her career to raise her children. She had a special needs child, so it ended up taking a few more years than she had planned. Now she wants to re-enter the work force, but she doesn't just want a job, she wants a career. She had a job at a college bookstore for a while, and she found that she was a bit jealous of the millennial mindset. Why can't she feel that hope and idealism—and have some of that tech-savvy, while we're at it? She's constantly worrying and wondering if it's too late for her."

"Then there's Paul. He's only 46, but he had a heart attack last autumn. He needs to find a new career. He and his partner are both corporate executive types. What is he going to do to replace the income to which they are accustomed that doesn't have stress? Or do they want to make a big lifestyle change? Like really big?"

Gladys shifts around in her seat, reaches underneath and pulls out a giant bag. She scrabbles inside until she grabs a Tupperware container, opens it and offers oatmeal raisin cookies. "Oh, honey, I'm not done. There are more kinds of people here in career crisis than you can imagine!" After she makes the cookies disappear, she starts in again.

"Chelsea is in a dream job. The problem is that it is someone else's dream job, not hers. It pays really well, great benefits, travel and lots of other perks. But they just don't seem so perky to her. She sits in meetings dreaming of being somewhere else...anywhere else. And she feels like a horrible person. Shouldn't she be able to be grateful? Her mother tells her that all the time! She should just be able to 'suck it up and be happy,' but she can't."

"Davida is overworked and underpaid. She does not love her work, but she's good at it. Deep down inside, she knows that if she does something about it, she's going to really stir up a hornet's nest—because she knows that it's really her marriage that's in trouble. She knows that if her marriage does come crashing down, she won't really be able to support herself and her son in her current job. But if she seeks a job that pays more and has more responsibility, it will shake up the precarious balance that's in place now. And if she works a lot, she can avoid thinking about it, right?"

"Next is Tim. His boss is a real jerk. Tim uses much more colorful language. His boss—let's call him Dick—thinks that it is perfectly appropriate to come into Tim's office and berate and insult him. Dick thinks that's motivational. He also thinks it's fair to withhold critical information, but still hold Tim accountable for results. There's a whole list of irrational and abusive behavior.

Tim took this job as a stepping stone in his career. On paper, it was a fantastic opportunity, but not in reality. The problem is that Tim is now so beaten down that he can't figure out a career move that makes sense. He doesn't have the confidence to put himself out there. Who knows what kind of disaster he'd be in an interview. How does Tim recover from this bad experience?"

"Leticia has been at her company for 14 years. She started out in her chosen profession. Over time, the company changed owners several times. There were a bazillion re-orgs. Now she is in a function that is nowhere near her area, doing stuff she hates, working for people that she detests (they are all probably relatives of Dick), in a culture that is horrid. How did that happen? She's pretty sure she's like the frog in the slowly heating pot. She just became acclimated to the changes gradually. How does she get out of this really crappy company filled with horrible people? And is her reputation so tarnished that she needs to find a totally different industry or career?"

"And there's Emma. She's all over the map. She makes good money doing what she does now, but she really doesn't like it. She wants something with more meaning, more creativity and variety. She wants to be more of a specialist. She wants that so desperately, but she can't find a career that suits her. And the more she wants it, the more elusive it seems. Oh yeah, and she actually doesn't believe she's qualified to do anything more than what she's doing—all evidence to the contrary. And she just got married. She wants babies—the clock is ticking! She just wants it all…and isn't sure she'll have anything."

"Pete has spent his whole life taking care of other people. He's a very hardworking health care provider. He's a wonderful provider for his family. But he's exhausted. He works in two practices and he does everything for everyone. He wants to live. He wants to write. He wants to do something that touches more people. What is that? And how does he get there from here?"

"Shall I go on?" she asks, but doesn't give you time to answer. "Paula has post-promotion depression, because getting the big promotion didn't make her as happy as she thought it would. She's at the top—now what? Where does she go from here? Jeff has your typical mid-career crisis. Should he change jobs or companies or careers or what? How does he face 20 more years of this? And Gina, well, she has a full blown crisis of faith going on. When she picked her career, she really had a calling. But things have changed so much, the *world* has changed so much over the past 10 years that she really doesn't know if she even wants to stay in it!"

Gladys wanders off to go find a drinking faucet or something, and finally gives you a moment's peace.

You take a moment to look around the room and realize that there are a whole bunch of different kinds of career crises. When you first came in, you kinda thought that a career crisis meant that you got fired and had to figure out what to do about it. But now you've either discovered that you're in a similar place to one of the people in the waiting room, or you have something very unique going on. But you wonder if you are really in *a crisis*. Well, you are if you think you are—it's that simple. But what kind of crisis? How big? How long will it last? How long will *you* last, before you pack it all in and become a barista. And why is being a barista the new dream job for the overly-stressed, high-powered executive, anyway? What kind of crisis are you in?

Is it all so overwhelming? Are you maybe feeling a little bit like Chelsea? Like you should just be grateful and suck it up and be happy where you are? Is your career crisis so important? With all the other stuff going on in the world today, how can you be so shallow as to focus on your career crisis. Hey—that's you saying that, not me!

Here's what I say. Career is important. It's your work. It might be your life's work. Or maybe not, but it's what you do. Look, we spend most of our adult life *at work*. That includes people who work at home, and it includes full-time parents. It is many hours of our waking life. Here's some math. There are 24 hours in a day, 168 hours in a week. Let's just pretend that you get 7 hours of sleep a day. That's 49 hours, so that leaves 119 waking hours. And let's also pretend that the average work week is 40 hours. (But we both know that isn't *your* average work week!) In this scenario, work is 33% of your waking life. You only have to get the number up to 60 hours to have it be **half** of your waking life. It doesn't take much to get up to 60 hours…especially if you travel or commute or work overtime, or bring your work home, or work on weekends, or "take a couple of calls", right? Some people think 10% is a big number—they like it when they get a 10% discount. So this is a big number. It should mean something to you.

In Western society, what we do is our identity; it's *who we are*. Think about it. Most of the time when we introduce ourselves, we announce our profession. It helps pigeon hole us. It's a real crisis for people who are out of work, for parents who have taken time off to raise children, for adult children who take time off to care for an aging parent or for anyone who just takes a break. Just ask them how hard it is to introduce themselves to strangers at a party, or how embarrassed they feel when they have to answer a simple question like, "so how's it going?"

A little more on the "you should just be grateful" topic. You tell yourself that you should just be grateful to have a job. Even if it doesn't make you happy. Even if it doesn't change the world. Even if whatever. Fine, yes. You should be grateful. But when did gratitude become greedy? I don't remember getting the memo that said you can *only* feel gratitude. You can actually feel both gratitude and any other emotion at the same time. You can be grateful that you have a job and still yearn to do something more meaningful, or less stressful, or higher paying or whatever it is that you are feeling. That's okay. You have my permission. You don't need it, but you have it. You see, that longing and yearning thing, that wanting more thing—it pushes you to *do and be* more. Gratitude is an awesome springboard. More on that later.

So we've established that career is an important topic. That means that dealing with what's going on with you and your career is also important. So how do we do that?

That's actually why I started out with the visual that you're waiting in a career crisis clinic with a bunch of other emergency cases. Initially we need to do some triage and treat the presenting symptoms. But we also need to do a thorough examination and diagnosis and get to the real cause. It'll be a bit like functional medicine. We'll look at the whole person and come up with a strategy to treat the root cause. Okay?

First, let's get you out of crisis mode. It's probably going to take a little first aid and maybe even some (gasp) self-care. Don't worry, we'll call it something else—and no, this book is not all about self-care. It is about how you craft a strategy to begin moving into your dream life—starting with your career. But you need to get your energy and perspective back so that you can focus. We need to get you off of adrenaline and pure emotion, and we need to get you out of fear and anxiety!!! So let's get some first-aid going.

To start, I prescribe the RICE treatment, because you can probably remember the acronym. For initial treatment of a sprain or strain, it stands for Rest, Ice, Compression and Elevation. For initial treatment of a career crisis, it stands for Rest, Intention,

Compassion, and Expectation. We will add some supplements in the next chapter.

R. Rest. Relax. Rejuvenate. Relief. You've come to the right place. You're going to be okay. You're not going to start jumping up and down on this thing with random action. You're going to rest and let the swelling and inflammation (aka fear and anxiety) go down. You'll get back into action mode, but you're going to do a few things first. The first thing is to start getting enough sleep. Mom was right when she said that it'll be better after a good night's sleep. And breathe!!! Add in some other things that help you relax and rejuvenate—maybe a soaky bath, a night out dancing, or a real weekend off. Whatever appeals to you. Set down the burden for a little bit, and know that when you come back to pick it up, you'll be better prepared to handle it.

I. Intention. Inquiry. Set an intention that you are going to figure this out, and you will absolutely end up with a strategy to get where you want to go. You will be inquisitive—asking the right questions and answering them honestly so that you discover what you need to know.

C. Compassion. Have compassion on yourself and your situation. You didn't get into this crisis on purpose. You aren't stuck here forever. Trust me when I tell you that yelling at yourself won't get you where you want to go any faster. So just stop it. And stop the judgy-judgy stuff, too. You're actually on your way to becoming a better, more compassionate person who is making a bigger difference in your world. Think of it as practice, and you are the guinea pig. It's okay, PETA. No real guinea pigs were used in this book.

E. Expectation. Expectation is a strong belief that something will happen or that someone will achieve something. It's stronger than hope. Start working on a positive expectation that you **will**

solve your career crisis: you will have clarity, a strategy, a plan and will take action to achieve it. Have realistic expectations that you will do it one step at a time, not all at once. You will have to do some work, but expect that it will be oh so worth it.

I have every confidence in you.

It's important to take a little time and do this RICE thing. You really can't just jump straight into action. It's so much better to have a plan. And a plan is so much better if you have a strategy. And a strategy is so much better if you have a clue. No, I mean, it's better if you have clarity. So that's what we're going to do. We're going to get you a strategy. Well, actually, that's what you're going to do. You have to do the work. I'd do it if I could, but that wouldn't do you any good at all. Besides, I've done it before, several times. That's part of how I know that it works. I've also done it with a whole bunch of clients.

You might have guessed that everyone in the waiting room has been a client of mine. Yup. I just changed their names. Every one of them is happier now than when they walked in, metaphorically speaking. You'll be hearing a lot more about them in the coming pages.

So it's not too hard, you can do it. You'll probably even enjoy doing it. I promise to try to make it fun!

• • • • • • • • • •
JOT SPOT
• • • • • • • • • •

Oh, did I catch you without some sticky notes??
Jot a quick note here, you can expand later in the workbook!

INTRODUCTION TO STRATEGY

"You can either set brick as a laborer or as an artist. You can make the work a chore, or you can have a good time. You can do it the way you used to clear the dinner dishes when you were thirteen, or you can do it as a Japanese person would perform a tea ceremony, with a level of concentration and care in which you can lose yourself, and so in which you can find yourself."
—Anne Lamott

This book is divided into a few parts. We're about to enter Part 1, which is an introduction to Strategy. I apologize, because I know it sounds a little condescending. You already know what the word "strategy" means, and you have probably had a whole bunch of opportunities in your life to "do strategy". But I'm going to do a little bit of level setting, to make sure we're on the same page. I'm sure I'll throw in some more buzz words along the way. I just want to make sure you know what I mean when I use the words, because it might be different from how you've used them before, and certainly it's a different context.

I'm also going to try to build a compelling case for why you need to spend time on your strategy before you do anything else—except the RICE stuff and some supplements. The what and why are important. We will get to the heart of the strategy work right after that. I know you want to jump to action. You want to feel like you are doing something, that you're making progress. Well you are doing something, and it's hella productive. You're getting prepped and you're getting in the zone.

I know you wanna click some buttons, rewrite your resume, apply for a job, sign up for a course. But resist the urge for just a little while longer. Try taking some supplements instead. According to Dictionary.com, a supplement is something added to complete a thing, supply a deficiency, or reinforce or extend a whole. So you are "the whole", and I am going to recommend that you add things to your life to compensate for a previous deficiency and to reinforce you.

Here is a list of my recommended supplements. It's by no means exhaustive. Of course you can put your own things on the list! I have to admit that I crowd-sourced the list. You can do that, too! Pick what appeals to you.

- Start hanging around with more positive people
- Go make something
- Bake bread—get your hands in there and knead the dough

- Plant things—touch dirt!
- Do something artistic. Find a short art class, where you walk away with something completed.
- Make or listen to some music
- Meditate
- Laugh. Smile. Play. Be silly.
- Daydream and doodle
- Do something absolutely brand new
- Do something scary (we'll talk more later)
- Sit through your emotions (don't avoid them)
- Take up a new sport or exercise for a week (Play, not perfect). Group exercise! Kick boxing. Something that really gets the stress out!
- Perform random acts of kindness
- Have a **real** conversation with a stranger
- Read a book for fun
- Get up early and watch the sun rise, or watch a sunset
- Breathe! Breathing exercises. Pausing. Big, deep, belly breaths.
- Take yourself on an artist's date (from the Artist's Way)
- Look up. Stop and look up at the clouds or the stars in the sky
- Go give. Go do something for others. Volunteer.
- Put. The Phone. Down.
- Go lie down on earth. Rest there. It's magic.
- Give yourself permission to do absolutely nothing.
- Go barefoot outside in the grass.
- Pet the cat (my kitty just came and sat on my lap with a loud "Meow" as if to remind me to not forget this very important one.)

Acknowledge someone for something—without any agenda, tell them what you see in them that's great about how they are and what they do. Do it as soon as you think of it: let them know that you know and appreciate this about them.

• • • • • • • • •
JOT SPOT
• • • • • • • • •

Oh, did I catch you without some sticky notes??
Jot a quick note here, you can expand later in the workbook!

Chapter 1

WHAT iS A STRATEGY?

• •

"The secret to having a rewarding work-life balance is to have no life. Then it's easy to keep things balanced by doing no work."
—**Scott Adams**, in a Dilbert cartoon

A Strategy is a method to bring about a desired goal or outcome. This book is about creating a personal strategy to get out of your career crisis, but actually, I want more than that for you. I don't want you to just get out of crisis, I want you to thrive, to be successful and to be happy. And not just in your career, in your life! So we're going to aim big. I'm going to have to do a little groundwork, first, so please be patient with me while I set a few things up for you in this chapter.

There are a couple of ways to do this book. I say "do this book" because there are a lot of exercises, questions and even visual

7

graphics that accompany this book, and you'll only end up with a strategy if you do them. You can choose to do them as you go along, or you can read the entire thing and then come back and do the exercises—either way works. I've created a companion workbook of the all exercises, which includes a visual for the exercise at the end of this chapter. You can get the workbook here http://www.ohsnap-thebook.com/. You have to sign up to be on my mailing list, and I'll send you occasional emails. I do recommend that you download the companion workbook right away, so that you have it while you go along.

I spent a long time in the corporate world. I learned a lot of really useful stuff. I also learned a lot of stuff that isn't very useful (bureaucracy) and became immune to the fact that a lot of it is unnecessary and highly irritating. I guess you could say that I became very unaware of my surroundings and the impact on their psyche. I babble about this because there is a chance that you are in the same state of mind. You no longer challenge things that need to be challenged. You are no longer irritated by the pile of things that should irritate you. You just step over them. You tolerate them. There's an exercise at the end of this chapter to help you change your perspective so that you can actually *see* the things that you've stopped seeing. It's eye opening. So don't skip the exercise.

Back to the part where I said I learned a lot of really useful stuff. You know that the corporate world spends a lot of time, energy and money figuring out how to do things better, right? Sometimes it's by trial and error, and there's nothing wrong with that if you actually pay attention to the error part and learn from it. Sometimes it's by research, and sometimes it's by listening to experts—both inside and outside the company. Companies profit when they are more effective so, for the most part they are motivated to improve. The term "best practices", might be overused, but it's a good concept. It means looking at what works and seeing if it can be copied or adapted somewhere else, and thereby reducing the learning curve. There's also a lot of emphasis on building skills and training. Then there's the concept of transferrable skills: across functions, roles, even across industries. I've learned lots about that, too. And you know what? We could totally take advantage of that corporate investment for our individual benefit, if we thought about it. We could transfer the skills we gain at work into our personal lives.

But we don't. In fact, I find that a lot of my clients spend a lot of energy keeping their work and personal lives separate, which actually contributes to their career crisis (more on that later). They don't take advantage of all the "work" skills that could help them achieve their goals for success and happiness in their own life. I have not heard much, if any, talk about taking what we learn in the business world and applying it to our personal lives. Why not? It makes sense, right? Many of the skills we learn in a business context are totally transferrable into our personal lives. Practical, tactical, soft, interpersonal, financial, planning—with a little tweaking, our personal lives could easily benefit from applying those skills. And wouldn't you just love to see some clear roles and responsibilities applied to the volunteer group you've joined? Wouldn't you love to see some meaningful metrics motivate your kid to improve their study habits? And wouldn't some best practices be nice to apply to the things that seem so hard to get done around the house? Don't you think some of the lessons learned in that big relocation project might help you think through your big household move? And what about a personal happiness plan, hey?

Why isn't there a discipline for taking skills from the business world and applying them elsewhere? Why isn't it a thing? Okay, from here on, it is a thing. I give you fair warning. I am absolutely going to leverage business stuff for your personal gain. Leverage, in this case, means steal.

Okay, besides the fact that there are some truly brilliant, timesaving things to steal, I have another reason for relying heavily on things I've learned in a corporate setting, and for making the connection to what's going on in your life. I want to help you tap into the part of your brain that has learned to follow processes, to make educated guesses, to solve problems and has a lot of observational data. I want you to be able to disconnect a bit from your personal "situation" so that you aren't as anxious and fearful and can come at it with some objectivity and different perspectives. This will give you some relief from the pressure—and from self-criticism. Yes, there will be times when you will need to be super in touch with your situation, thoughts and feelings. But not all the time. So using business language, metaphors and skills helps you to quickly move to an objective point of view, where you aren't reacting, you're thinking. And strategy is all about thinking. Actually, it's all about awareness. Okay, it's gonna be all about whatever point I'm making at the time I'm trying to make it.

Now that I've explained why I will go back and forth between "business" language and "personal development" language, let's get into the definition of a strategy in this context—the personal context of being in a career crisis. We need a personal strategy to get out of the crisis. (Actually, *you* need it, but that's the next chapter.)

First thing to know: a strategy is not a plan! This is important, because a lot of times we confuse strategy with something called a strategic plan. And that's just an excuse to jump into action. If you jump straight into action, the chances are really high that you are either going to a) make a mess that you have to untangle or b) run around ineffectively, wasting a lot of time and energy. You can't get the time back, you know.

So here is our first use of transferable skills—taking something from the world of business and translating it so that it is useful in our personal world; let's look at strategy in business. There can be different levels of strategy, and they need to be aligned to be successful. The corporate strategy is overarching. The component parts of the organization—business divisions, functional units, teams and individuals—all have strategies and goals that support the corporate strategy.

So to translate from business into life, you might have an overarching life strategy, and supporting strategies that focus on the areas of career, family, health, lifestyle, etc. Chances are you haven't thought in these terms, and the idea of a "family strategy" seems cold and calculating. It's just semantics. In reality, you've probably always had an idea of whether or not you wanted to marry, have children, how many you wanted and when, what kind of home you wanted to live in, etc. You've probably had hopes and dreams for all of these things. Life has probably thrown you a couple of curve balls, but that's exactly why you need a strategy… next chapter.

So what you want in life, that's your life strategy. Maybe it's really well thought out, maybe not. But when you really know what you want, you know what steps to take to make it happen, right? That's a strategy.

This book is about your personal strategy to get out of your career crisis, with a few other related items thrown in. The first—and most important thing to realize is that your career is just one facet of your life, and you want to think of it in context. That means that your career strategy needs to be seen in context of your life strategy. So in reality, you're going to define your life strategy first, then how your career strategy fits in. The next thing you need to know is that because your career strategy is intimately related to your life strategy, there is no one-size-fits-all career strategy—no matter what anyone says—your parents, your boss, that snippy high school guidance counselor back in the day, or anyone else who wants to weigh in! Your career strategy is unique to you.

Okay, back to work here. Corporate strategy generally answers the question "what do we need to do to win in our market?" and drives the direction, scope, structure, objectives and decisions for an organization.

Great, let's translate that. "What do I need to do to have a successful and happy life?" Remember, this is *your* definition of success, not someone else's. So your strategy is going to answer *that* question, and it will help you make decisions, take actions, set goals, identify and build foundations and structure that steer your life in that direction. A strategy helps you to identify your north star, so that you can make sure that the actions you take move you in the right direction. Once you know your overall strategy, you develop a career strategy that supports and enables your life strategy.

Choosing your strategy—your direction—means that there is some risk involved, because you are really just guessing at what lies ahead. You've heard people say "take a SWAG", right? Well the "s" usually stands for scientific (Wild *ssed Guess). We're going to change it to "strategic", but it's still a bit of a guess and a risk. You are choosing something(s), and deciding not to go with something(s) else. The irony is that while there is a risk that you might make some incorrect guesses when developing your strategy, one of the best ways to mitigate risks is to have a clear strategy and adjust it!

Maybe you've had difficulty making decisions in the past, out of fear that you might get it wrong. Or you suffer from analysis paralysis. You take few, if any, actions. (Which, by the way is the passive-aggressive style of making choices!) Or perhaps you make an absolutely completely comprehensive plan, which pretty much locks you in. Well, a strategy is a choice, but you can adjust along the way. You've probably heard the quotes about planes being off course most of the time, and that piloting is really a series of course corrections. Your life is like that, too, and you will be able to handle what life throws at you—including the career bumps, tailwinds and headwinds—waaay more effectively if you have a navigational strategy.

There are lots of ways to craft a strategy. I'm going to walk you through my way. It's not the only way. I think my process is the best, just like Ricky Gervais thinks that he does the best celebrity imitations in the world. https://www.youtube.com/watch? v=SLMLPPFK7m8 Okay, not *just* like that. Anyway, we'll get to the "how" in Chapter 3. But next up, I'll spend a little time telling you "why" a strategy is the first thing you should do.

Meanwhile, let's go to the tolerations exercise.

Tolerations Exercise

We tend to get dragged down and overwhelmed by things that accumulate over time—and end up cluttering our minds. Now is the time to identify what you're tolerating!

Tolerations are like pearls. They start out as irritations—things that rub us the wrong way, irritate us, hurt, distract or keep us stuck. But we don't get rid of them, we get used to them. We build a buffer or a coating somehow, that makes them less irritating. We become blind to them. The rough edges smooth out enough that we can work around them. They take up space, but they don't exactly hurt anymore. But like pearls, they don't belong inside our perimeter, our shell. When we take them out, we can actually see how big they are, and they become beautiful because they are outside.

What are the things that you tolerate? Make a list. You may not want to do anything about them right now, but just writing them out will raise your awareness and you'll naturally start handling, fixing and resolving them.

Examples could be: Incomplete tasks, frustrations, problems, other people's or your own behavior, clutter, shoulds (or shouldn'ts), unmet needs, crossed boundaries, overdue library books/DVDs, outdated wardrobe, unresolved issues or guilt, lack of exercise, eating habits, being indecisive, procrastinating, lack of sleep, etc.

In Summary

- A lot of resources are spent figuring out the best ways to do things in the business world.
- We can totally leverage those learnings in our personal life.
- When we tap into our "business brain" we can separate ourselves from some of the emotional impact of our career crisis.
- We want a strategy to help guide us to achieve success and happiness in our lives, which I call a life strategy.
- Our career is a facet of our life, so we need a separate strategy, a career strategy, that aligns and supports our life strategy.
- We'll be looking at both in this book.

JOT SPOT

Oh, did I catch you without some sticky notes??
Jot a quick note here, you can expand later in the workbook!

Chapter 2

YOU NEED A STRATEGY

• •

"I choose a lazy person to do a hard job. Because a lazy person will find an easy way to do it."
—Bill Gates

I actually say something similar. "I like to hire people who are smart and lazy, because they'll come up with a strategy to get it done once and make it repeatable."

Now we're going to talk about why you need a strategy. This is a pretty short chapter, so even if you already know why, please read it. I might say something new, or it might spur you to think of something I haven't mentioned. Either way, you're going to need a powerful "why" to keep you motivated to actually do the work and to be honest with yourself so that you have a great strategy that fits what you really want. Because

I can tell you right now that you will probably be tempted to just skip the strategy and jump straight to action at some point. And that would be a real shame, because you do need a strategy. Remember, it's your North Star, a vision of the future you want to create, and it's there for directional guidance and the occasional course correction. Is there a more powerful "why" than creating the future you want? By the way, you can have several goals in your strategy!

Here's my big list of reasons why you need a strategy, in no particular order:

- If you don't have a strategy, you're going to jump into semi-random action. It's like throwing spaghetti at the wall and hoping that what sticks will be a work of art. It won't be. It'll be a mess. Maybe a Picasso-esque mess, but it'll still be a bunch of work to clean up.
- Your career is valuable and you want to look professional. Random action does not treat your career as if it's valuable. Going on the wrong interviews, having the wrong resume for the role, having a mismatched LinkedIn profile, changing directions frequently, stammering through conversation with the headhunter about what you're looking for...not so professional looking.
- You don't want to waste time on a lot of ineffective action. That's the scattershot approach. Without a strategy and a plan, you end up in reaction mode, instead of being proactive. It's exhausting and disheartening.
- You don't want your actions to take you in a wrong direction. Without spending the time to really think through what you want, it's easy to get off course. Something can seem like a wonderful direction, a fantastic opportunity. Maybe

it is. Maybe it is for someone else. How do you know if you haven't figured out what the right direction is?

- You don't want to be completely lost if something happens that upsets the apple cart. Because there's the whole "life happens" thing. Not everyone can be Forest Gump, turning each unexpected event into some special kind of lemonade. As I mentioned before, a strategy helps you get back on course when something gets you off course. You can always adjust your plans, even your goals.

- You don't want habit or inertia to take you back to where you started. It's a sneaky thing. When you aren't really clear on where you want to go, after a while it doesn't seem quite so bad to stay where you are.

- You don't want to write a prescription without really diagnosing the problem. That's kinda what action without a strategy is. You'll end up treating the symptoms, and finding yourself back in the same situation in a few months—or worse!

- You don't want to fix the wrong problem. This is related to the point above, but slightly different. Is it your job, your role, the company, your career? Is it something else completely? Are you looking at your career, when there's really something else in your life that's the cause of your dissatisfaction? You know, like when a new convertible and an affair seem like the perfect answer to a mid-life crisis.

- Your career is part of your whole life and you want it to support your life. Taking a look at what you want out of your life—in many facets—will help you to make sure that your career goals are aligned with your life goals. It's such a simple concept, but many of my clients have lost sight of it. It didn't happen all at once, it's a gradual thing that happens over time. Getting it back into their awareness has led to fundamental shifts and dramatic progress.

- You want to be able to recognize opportunities when they come across your path, right?... to know pretty quickly whether something aligns with your goals or not.

- You want to be able to tell that you are making progress, especially over the duration of your career. Getting out of crisis is one thing, but progressing toward your goal is something different.

- What about knowing that you've achieved your goal? If you aren't clear about what it is, you won't know. You might want to say, "awesome, we're here, and I don't really have any further ambitions, because I like my life like this." Or you might say, "right, time to update my strategy with some new goals!"

Once you have your strategy, you can make a plan. The strategy is the desired outcome. The plan is a tactical set of actions, milestones and metrics—that's how you achieve your strategy. You make a plan because you want to get something done, you want to be successful and you want to be able to sleep at night because you know what you have to do next.

Let's look at a couple of very realistic scenarios. One without a strategy, one with.

Scenario 1, No strategy: You are unhappy in your current job. You should have had a promotion a while ago. Younger people keep getting promoted around you. You're getting more and more frustrated. You're thinking about changing jobs, roles, companies, even careers. One day you feel extraordinarily frustrated, you've had enough and you are going to do something. So you set off a chain reaction of random actions—you call a headhunter friend, you send your resume (as is) to a listing you kinda like, you go on an interview for something that might be "interesting", etc. Most of these actions go nowhere (or nowhere you really want to go) and you've spun around in a futile whirl of activity—and you become disheartened. Not to mention that you haven't done things in a logical order, with thought and cohesion, missing a step or two. You have to backtrack with your headhunter. You've created a whole list of things to do around making a change, but you really don't know what you want to change or what direction. So you end up creating five different versions of your resume, to fit five plausible scenarios…just in case. You've completely fallen into this scattershot approach. You're wasting a lot of time and you come across as unfocused. You could be so much more effective if you knew what you wanted, thought through what you wanted to say and how to position yourself, addressed any gaps, created your supporting collateral and pursued it with laser focus…and that's if you really did want to make a change!

Scenario 2, you've started on your strategy: You know that you want to make a change and you've articulated some of the things that are important to you. You know that you're ready for a new, bigger challenge. You really want more responsibility and the authority you need to be successful. You want to move to a smaller organization, because you want more hands-on interaction and to be more of a generalist. You want to reduce your commute, because you're missing way too many soccer games and concerts and pizza nights. You've worked out what kind of salary you want to make, and what kind of trade-offs you'd be willing to make.

One day, a former colleague calls you out of the blue, to ask if you know of anyone who might be interested in a senior management role in a small local company. They aren't thinking of you, but they know that you know a lot of people in the industry.

But it actually sounds interesting to you. Because you've spent time thinking through what you want, you recognize it as a potential opportunity. You know what questions to ask to see how well it fits with your strategy. Before you put in the thought, you would have either never seen it as an opportunity for yourself or would have agonized about whether or not it was the right move. How awesome to have your North Star.

Making It Real

Here's a real life example. Remember Tim from the waiting room? It's okay if you don't—there were a lot of people in the waiting room. Tim's the guy with colorful speech, and he worked for Dick, the horrible boss. Tim had taken a job that looked perfect on paper—it was a step up in title, responsibility and pay, and he figured he would be there for several years as he positioned himself to step up to the top job. Yeah, that was on paper. In real life, Dick made his life a living torture chamber. He had all the responsibility and none of the authority. Dick changed the rules frequently, and pretty much insulted Tim on a personal level when Dick needed something to make himself feel better. One day Tim finally reached his breaking point. He knew that he was either going to be fired any day now or he was going to explode and then get himself fired. He couldn't really afford to do that, because he and his wife had just bought a new house and were in the process of selling their old one. So to try to maintain some job security, he kept trying harder to please his boss, which of course didn't work because Dick was a bully. The constant stress undermined Tim's self-confidence. Tim did not see this ending well, so he decided that he would get a coach (me!). The first thing we did was a little first-aid to relieve the immediate pressure. Once Tim could confirm that he really wasn't going to get fired, he was able to relax a bit and work on his strategy, following the process you'll see in the next section. He knew that he did not have to find something else out of desperation, and that he would be the one who decided when and how he would leave. With a clear picture of what is important to him in his career and his life, Tim now talks coherently to headhunters about what he's looking for; he knows which interviews to go on and he interviews from a place of confidence. He has learned that culture, leadership and ethics are very important to him, and he has crafted his list of questions to take to an interview, too! Most importantly, he has figured out how he can get along in his current job long enough to find the right career move that aligns with his career and life strategy.

Making It Yours

So hopefully you see all the reasons why you need a strategy. But let's make sure it isn't a completely intellectual or theoretical exercise. Take a few moments to reflect and answer these questions. Yeah, write it down. Get used to it. You're going to be doing a lot of that.

- Think of a time or two when you jumped straight to action, without a plan or a strategy. How did that work out for you—did you get what you wanted? What worked, what didn't? What did you learn?

- Identify the ways that having a strategy and a plan might have changed the outcome. What could you do differently?

- Think of a time (preferably in a work context) where you did follow a process to develop a strategy, plan and executed against the plan. You might have been part of the team, or you might have been an observer. What worked, what didn't? What did you learn?

- Can you see how you could translate that experience into transferrable skills that apply to your personal life? It's okay if it doesn't completely translate.

- Get specific now. In your current career crisis, what is likely to happen if you don't have a strategy?

- How important is it to you to use this career crisis as an opportunity to develop a strategy?

A strategy is not a magic bullet. But all the thought that you put into creating your strategy, that *is* magic!

· · · · · · · · · ·
JOT SPOT
· · · · · · · · ·

Oh, did I catch you without some sticky notes??
Jot a quick note here, you can expand later in the workbook!

CREATING A STRATEGY

Now you are almost ready to start the work of creating your strategy. I'll give you a high level introduction here, so that you know what to expect. I'll also give you some tips on how to prepare, and how to stay focused.

First, let's talk about preparation. I don't think I need to tell you to take this process seriously, because I bet that's your natural inclination. I mean, it's important, right? So naturally you put on your serious face. I bet that I do need tell you to lighten up and have fun with it. Lighten up—that's such a wonderful phrase, and it can be taken so many ways: ease the burden, drop some unnecessary heaviness, don't be so serious, add some humor, add some illumination, turn on the lights and step lightly to rattle off just a few interpretations. Dropping the burden of excess heaviness makes the journey easier; you can almost imagine skipping or maybe even dancing. Adding light makes it easier to see clearly and get rid of the shadows; you can see what's really there instead of what you imagine might be hiding in the dark. Adding a little levity makes it much more enjoyable, and that will make it much easier to have a bright and hopeful vision. So lighten up!

Another bit of preparation—gather the materials you'll need. That will include a notebook or journal and a bunch of Sticky notes. I recommend the super-sticky kind of Post-its, but any kind of sticky note will work, so that you can move them around, but it's not mandatory. You can use any brand you like, too, of course. I also recommend that you get a notebook that you like, but not so much that you won't write in it.

Download the bonus materials from my website. I've included some tools that will make this easier. I like doing visual exercises, so I've created a few of those. www.ohsnap-thebook.com/

I highly recommend adding a habit like Julia Cameron's Morning Pages to your daily routine while you are working on your strategy. They are such a wonderful way to clear out the stream of consciousness thoughts (aka junk) and to get the creative thought processes going. It's like a daily warm up for the mind voice. Basically, first thing in the morning, you write longhand for three pages. Morning Pages are an exercise from *The Artist's Way* http://juliacameronlive.com/basic-tools/morning-pages/.

Stake out a space where you feel comfortable, can be free from distractions and you can leave things up on the wall so that you can look at them. You'll want to be able to add thoughts, move things around, sit and stare and really *live* with your thoughts and ideas. You can add things to the space that help you set your intention—quotes, candles, pictures, even a vision board—whatever works for you. If you can't claim a physical space, make a portable workspace. Get a binder and get some ledger-size paper or a large drawing pad. You can stick stickies to pages as virtual walls.

Finally, pick something that will work as a "starting ritual". It's the action that you'll take before you start, each time you sit down to do the work on your strategy. It can be making a cup of tea and putting your phone on mute, or lighting a candle, doing a breathing exercise. Whatever you choose, it needs to be something that tells you "I'm doing *this* now." Then set a specific intention—in your own words—about what you want to accomplish for that work session. Setting an intention helps you focus on—and achieve—your goal. Wayne Dyer said, "Our intention creates our reality." If you lose focus or hit something difficult or become distracted, you can call up the intention again to refocus. Try it. It works.

Next, let's talk a little about the process of creating a strategy. Yes, it's a process. There's always a process as far as I'm concerned. I find it reassuring. I love knowing what the process is, because then I don't feel quite so lost. It's almost as if I have a map that I can read. Actually, I do create process maps, because I'm a bit visual. So I'll do that now for you.

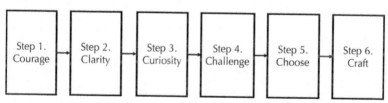

These are the steps of the process. Each step is a chapter, with instructions and explanations, real life stories, probing questions and exercises. As you work your way through each step, you flesh out the elements of your strategy, and pull them together in the last step.

Step 1. Courage—Use your courage muscle to take charge of your career and your life.

Step 2. Clarity—Get clarity on what you want for your life, and how your career fits in.

Step 3. Curiosity—Research and explore your options with curiosity and objectivity.

Step 4. Challenge—Call out your assumptions and challenge them.

Step 5. Choose—Make choices based on *your* priorities.

Step 6. Craft—Pull the elements of your strategy together into a cohesive document.

Chapter 3

STEP 1. COURAGE:
TAKE THE LEAD
• • • • • • • • • • • • • • • •

**Use your courage muscle to take charge
of your career and your life**

We are blown by the wind
Just like clouds in the sky
We don't know where we're going,
Don't know why
We just ride with the wind
And we'll drive through the rain
We don't know where we'll get to
Or if we'll get back again
Blown by the Wind
—from the Alan Parsons Album *On Air*

The quote above is a fragment of lyrics from a song off of On Air, a richly textured art album about the history of airborne exploration. The context of the whole song is about following your heart and not being tied down by the weight of empty material possessions. It's worth listening to the entire song! I've taken just a portion of lyrics out of context, to make a point. As it usually happens when a quote is taken out of context, it distorts the original meaning from when it was in context. (Can you say "Bible?")

Honestly, I don't think you want to live your life just blown about by the wind. Or maybe you do. It sounds like a wonderful way to take a vacation, to escape responsibilities. Or maybe that's how your life has been up to this point. You feel like you've just kinda fallen into things, blown about by circumstances "beyond your control". Okay. But if it isn't how you want to live the **rest** of your life, if you want to have some say in the direction your life takes instead of being a victim of the metaphorical wind, then you need to take the reins. Wait, wouldn't it be more consistent to say "take the helm?" I warn you now, I do love the mixology of metaphors. Let me take that particular sailboat metaphor a little further. The wind is a powerful force, right? You want it to fill your sails and take you where you want to go. But unless you're harnessing and directing the wind—steering the ship—you are likely to end up somewhere you don't really want to be!

Remember how in the introduction I said that I liked to steal… ahem… leverage some of those business learnings? Well, I want to do that right away. Like now. I want to look at the attributes of a strong C-level executive. Because, let's face it, if you are going to be in charge of your life, then you need to be in charge! You are the executive team that runs your life. You are the CEO, which in this case stands for the Chief Everything Officer. You are the head of operations, finance, marketing, information, security, innovation, et cetera, et cetera. Your life and career deserve the kind of C-Suite thought leadership that is often reserved for the business realm. In order to develop a strategy, you need to step into the role of CEO.

So let's start by looking at seven attributes of a strong C-level exec to see what we can leverage. You don't need to narrow it down to a career or industry, because for C-level leadership, you don't need technical, functional or even industry specific expertise as much as you need some other key strengths. And you don't need to be distracted by some of the not-so-nice aspects of the C-level life: things like enormous egos, living your life in meetings, having more work than one person could possibly do, and never knowing the satisfaction of task completion. Let's just take what we want and leave the rest. Here are the seven specific strengths that I recommend you take on, in the role of CEO of your life.

1. **Be visionary.** A CEO needs a clear vision and perspective. You have to have a high level vision of what you want out of life, what you want to achieve, to include, to experience, to share, to make, to do, to feel. As CEO you are responsible for making sure that you have a cohesive vision, and that it is **your** vision for **your** life.

2. **See the big picture.** The C-level execs look at the issues on the table in the context of the whole picture, not in isolation. Your life—as a whole—is the big picture. Your career, while important, is just one component of your life. You need to be able to keep the larger objectives and long term goals in mind, and maintain balance between all the different areas of your life. You are responsible for making sure all of the details line up in the direction you want to go.

3. **Prioritize**. Strong leaders set clear priorities and use them to make decisions. As CEO of you, you need to be able to set priorities, to recognize when there are competing priorities, resolve the conflicts, and reset the direction when things get off track.

4. **Rely on others**. A strong leader knows that he or she doesn't know everything, and that on occasion you need to call in some outside experts. They have a network, they establish partnerships. They build a team, and they know when to delegate. As CEO of you, you need to cultivate trustworthy advisors, partners and competent support. You need to know when to listen, and when to speak, and when to ask for help.

5. **Take appropriate risks.** Any CEO knows that there are times when they have to take risks. Risks are unavoidable. They want to minimize, mitigate, and manage. Ultimately, though, choices have to be made, and risks have to be taken. So as CEO of you, you need to have the ability and willingness to take appropriate risks and to know what "appropriate" means for you!

6. **Make difficult Decisions**. C-level executives make decisions all the time—that's really the bulk of their job. And many of those decisions are hard and unpopular. Likewise, you have to be able to make the critical decisions and the difficult choices, making sure that they are in line with your vision and priorities.

7. **Be a leader**. Great C-Suiters make bold and brilliant moves. They recognize opportunities, seek good advice, take appropriate risks, and make difficult decisions that align with their vision and priorities. That's what you need

to do to be CEO. You own and lead your own life, as well as your career.

The point is to change your perspective. As you create your strategy, I suggest that you intentionally grab the big leadership role, hold the perspective that you are the CEO of your life, and deliberately cultivate the 7 strengths. Which is a really good start, but…

…but there's one more strength: **courage**. Courage is the ability or power to do something that is frightening or difficult. It's strength in the face of fear or pain or difficulty. Courage is a muscle, and it needs to be worked. You can build your courage muscle with strength and flexibility training. It takes practice and consistency. And when you do build your courage muscle, you have the advantage of muscle memory! You remember how to be courageous. Courage isn't really a strength that comes out of the business world. In fact, it really comes from our life experiences. But it is absolutely necessary when it comes to creating our strategy, because it takes some big bravery to take charge of our own life and career, to claim responsibility for our decisions and our actions. It's easy to follow someone else's direction or to blow the way the wind blows. It's scary to take the lead…what if you're wrong?

It's okay to be afraid. You can still be courageous, in spite of fear. Fear can be very useful. At this stage in our evolution, fear plays a different role than it did eons ago. Oh sure, it does tell us that our life might be in danger when we see a bear or a lion. We get the squirt of adrenaline that we need to handle life threatening situations. But these days, most of the times we feel fear, we are not actually in physical danger. These days, our fears are more often in response to a belief that something or someone we love or value is threatened. If we take a moment to stop and look at the fear, we can use it to help us understand what is really important to us, and what the perceived danger is. We can decide whether the threat is real, or whether it's a misperception. And then we can decide what to do about it. And the doing probably takes courage, because the fear doesn't just go away.

You build your courage muscle just like you would any other muscle. You don't start by doing the biggest, scariest thing you can think of—that's just asking for an injury. You need to start by lifting smaller "weights" to build your strength and endurance, and throw in some variety for flexibility (see the exercises for the Courage CrossFit workout).

So don't wait. Don't be passive. You are in charge. Work on your courage muscle.

Making It Real

Remember Mitch? He's the guy who sort of stumbled into a job in the financial world. And he sort of stayed there for 22 years. It wasn't all bad, by any means. When the company relocated, he took a package. That bought him some time. And now, he wants to take control of his life. He doesn't want to default back to what he did before. He wants to make some changes, so that his career and his job allow him to have more of what he wants out of life, and less of what he doesn't. He doesn't want to commute an hour or more to and from work every day. He doesn't want to sit in a cubicle, in front of a computer screen all day every day. He does want to make some big changes.

Mitch is actively working to develop the seven skills. He is currently working on his vision for his whole life, with work being one part of it. He knows that he needs to set his priorities and actually make choices based on them. He is fully aware that there might be a difficult decision or two (or three or four) to be made. He is practicing.

Most importantly, Mitch has been working on his courage muscle. He has been doing one thing that scares him every day. Initially, he was surprised by the types of things that scared him. They were mostly about talking to people, re-connecting, reaching out for help or advice. His M.O. was to just avoid. But when he looked into the fear he discovered that he was afraid of things like awkwardness or how he appeared to others, because relationships really matter to him. He recognized that some of it stemmed from being out of practice, and that by practicing, he really was building his courage muscle. Gradually increasing the "weight", he's become much more comfortable doing uncomfortable things! That's taking the lead.

Making It Yours

In each of these "working" chapters, I'll give you something to make sure it isn't an entirely theoretical exercise. Let's make this about you. So think about these questions, write down your answers.

1. First let's evaluate: How in charge have you been of your life lately? Are you the leader, or have you been blown by the wind? How do you like your answer? What do you want for the next stage of your life?

2. How visionary are you? Do you have a clear picture of what you want out of life?

3. Do you see the big picture? Do you have long term goals and objectives, or are you managing life one day/week/month at a time? Do you integrate the different aspects of your life?

4. Can you prioritize? Do you know what your priorities are? Did you pick them, or were they picked for you (by life, by someone else, etc.)? Can you actually say what your #1 priority is? #2?

5. Do you feel like you need to do everything for yourself, or can you rely on others? Do you ask for help when you need it? Do you delegate? Do you have trusted advisors or

mentors or a coach? Do you have any real partnerships in your life?

6. How are you with taking risks? Do you know what is appropriate for you? Is it really hard for you to take calculated risks, or are you a gambler? Does it depend? Upon what? Are you good at thinking through potential issues and mitigating them?

7. Can you make difficult decisions? How does it feel when you do? Do you agonize? Do you revisit? Do you decide and move on? Do you delay until they are made for you? What's your process for making difficult decisions? Do you learn from the decisions you make? Even the mistakes?

8. Are you a leader? How well do you embody and integrate all of these strengths? Do you make bold moves when it's the right thing to do? Do you feel like a leader? Do you feel like you are/can be/will be the CEO of your life?

How about your career? Your health? Any other aspects of your life?

Exercise: Cultivate the 7 strengths

Look over your answers to the questions above. If there is something about your answer that you want to change, think about what you want to **do** about it. What strengths do you want to work on? Now remember the whole lighten up thing. If you want to change something, try to find a way to make it easy and fun. It doesn't have to hurt. In fact, you probably won't do anything about it if it's too hard, right? You can start small and work your way up, just like with the courage muscle.

Here's a hint: you can "act as if". Yup, that's right. You can be a method actor, find your motivation, get into character. You can step into the skin of the future you. Whatever works for you. Ask yourself, "If I really were the person who was in charge of my life, what would I do?" Then do that thing. Practice on the little things. Then bigger things. Then when it's time for the really big things, you already know how to do it!

• • • • • • • • •
JOT SPOT
• • • • • • • • •

Oh, did I catch you without some sticky notes??
Jot a quick note here, you can expand later in the workbook!

Chapter 4

STEP 2. CLARITY

• • • • • • • • • • • • • • • • •

Get clarity on what you want for your life, and how your career fits in

"Clarity takes time. It's not something you think about in one instant and have it. True clarity requires exploration of the details that surround what you want and often a few revisions to put all the puzzle pieces together. The #1 reason I see people don't get what they want is they don't invest the time it takes to get clear."
—**Cassie Parks**, Bestselling Author & LOA Lifestyle Design Coach

Albert Einstein said, "If I had an hour to solve a problem I'd spend 55 minutes thinking about the problem and 5 minutes thinking about solutions." That's the best way to make sure that the solution actually addresses the problem you're trying to solve! It's so tempting to jump to action without a strategy, which makes it waaaay too easy to solve the wrong problem! So to make sure that doesn't happen, the second step is all about getting clarity: about the problem, about what you want, what's important to you, what kind of outcome you want and what you believe the constraints are. You need to know all that stuff if you are going to have a strategy that actually makes a difference in your life. Oh, right…in your life. I said that. Because here it is. Your career is just one facet of your life. It is important for all the reasons we've already talked about. But I remind you again, that your career is **not** your life, and you are **not** your career, no matter how much you have been defined by it up to this point. The strategy you are going to develop for your career is going to be part of, align with and support what you want out of life. So we start by getting clarity about what you want out of your life, right?

So clarity. Here's why: You don't just sit down and invent a strategy. Well, you could, but 99.9999 times out of 100, it would be crap. To rephrase, you don't just invent a *good* strategy. And you want a good strategy, because it's going to help you to navigate life and what it throws at you and to keep going in the direction you want to go. You develop a strategy to be proactive, not reactive. You develop a strategy to address real and potential challenges, issues and opportunities. You probably haven't thought about **all** of the things that will play into your strategy, at least recently. You've thought about some of the things, sure.

Clarity doesn't just happen, as Cassie said in the quote above. It takes time. The good news is that you have a bit more than the hour Einstein allotted in his quote. So in this step, you are going to set some time aside to think, answer questions and write down the answers. You're going to take time to figure out a bunch of things that you need to know before you pick a direction. Clarity is a decision; you decide what you do and don't want. So you need to research and think and investigate and think some more. You intuit, guess, ask advice and think some more. You make some decisions. You ask a lot of questions—of yourself and people you respect. You take time, but you don't sit around and just wait for clarity to come to you; you pursue it. Now that doesn't mean that you need to devote a big chunk of time all at once to answering these questions. It actually works better if you work a little, go do something else and let the questions steep for a while, come back do a little more, sleep, come back...you get the picture. It's kinda like making risotto. You simmer, stir, add some stuff, stir, add more water, stir some more and keep doing it until you have some sticky deliciousness. Yes, I know that risotto isn't clear. Don't be so literal!

Clarity is a state of mind, too, where you have the ability to think clearly. So as you are taking this time to get clarity, make sure to take time to be clear. Pay attention to what makes you feel fuzzy and unclear and crowd them out of your life (temporarily or permanently, you decide), by adding in more of the things that make you feel clear and healthy. These can be people, food, drink, exercise, emotions, circumstances, places, almost anything. Crowd out the toxins by adding in what feeds you.

When you are properly cleaned up and ready for a clarity pursuing session, settle in and answer these questions. Be honest, but don't be mean. You'll know when you're finished answering the question. If it's a struggle, try to be curious and free from judgment. Why is it hard to answer? Come at it from a different perspective. Sometimes the difficult ones are the best ones to mine, because they are rich with ore, or jewels, or whatever you're mining! Or maybe you're mushroom hunting, to add to the risotto! There is no single "correct" answer. The right answers are the ones that resonate with you, that make you say "yes, that *feels* right, that *feels* true for me."

Oh yeah, one more thing. As you begin to answer these questions, you're going to start getting ideas, and many of them won't have anything to do with what you're doing. Yup, it just happens. Maybe you want to keep them, maybe you'll toss them later. Don't waste your time deciding right now. Park 'em in the Parking Lot. Here's how: Pick a wall or a big sheet of paper that you don't need right now and call it the Parking Lot. When you get ideas that aren't on topic, write them down on Sticky notes and park 'em. You could just make a list, but the psychology of sticky notes is interesting—great for ideas and inspiration, because there is so little commitment. We'll get into that more a little bit later. For now, just write enough to know what you're talking about and park 'em. Then go back to what you were doing.

Okay, now you can start. Dig into these questions. It's totally okay if you add your own or follow tangents to see how they play out. Your answers can be for any facet of your life, including, but not limited to your career!

What's the problem, exactly? Understand it. Describe it. Like the Einstein quote above, spend enough time to be clear about what you're trying to figure out! Your career is in some kind of crisis, so get clear on the crisis. What's going on? Be specific. Was there a single event that precipitated the crisis, has it been building or is it a general state of malaise? Is it your job, the culture, the company? Is it your boss? Is it you? Just maybe? Is it a lack of growth, challenge, progress? Is it too hard, too demanding or just too much work? Has your life changed and your current career—or job—doesn't work anymore? It's okay if you come up with more than a couple of things. You can have a multi-faceted crisis! Remember, the better you understand your situation and what isn't working for you, the better you will be able to create a strategy that fits!

What are you feeling? What emotions? What physical feelings? How are they tied together? Don't discount this question! It can give you some information you haven't been "thinking" about, because you're probably functioning on autopilot most of the time. Or worse, you've built up a tolerance and have stopped paying attention to the truths that your feelings could tell you. You might have conflicting feelings. Chances are pretty good that fear is in there somewhere.

What do you want? Broadly, like in your whole life. Go spend 20 minutes writing an "I want rant" and don't stop until you can't think of another thing that you want. What do you yearn for? It can be a thing, a feeling, an experience, a state of mind... pretty much anything. For inspiration, you can do the Web of Life exercise at the end of this chapter. After you've finished with your life as a whole, you can move on to your job and/or your career, and get very specific. How do you want to spend your day? What do you want in terms of company culture? What kind of people do you want to work with? What kind of recognition? What kind of challenges? How much money do you want? What kind of tasks do you want to do? Do you have a title in mind? How do you want to feel? There's lots to explore here, so invent your own questions. Another way to ask is "what's calling you?"

What's important? What's not important? You might want to revisit your answers from the previous question and pick out what's most and least important from there, or maybe this question prompts a whole different set of answers. Whether you believe you can have it all or not, the chances are that you are going to have to compromise. At the very least, you need to prioritize because you'll have choices. Your strategy is going to guide you in actions

AND in decisions. So get clear about what you are not willing to give up and what you are. The answers might surprise you— just make sure that they are YOUR answers. Once you have the answers, pick the top 5 to 10 things that are important to you and write them on Sticky notes. Now do a forced ranking by sticking them in order, most important at the top. These are your priorities. Hang on to this list, because you are going to use it later. Yes, of course you can change your mind. You can change the order of importance. You can move them around. You can swap one out. That's why you wrote them on Sticky notes!

What are you worried about? What are the thoughts that are keeping you awake at night? What are the questions that you really wish you could answer right now? Who, What, When, Where, Why are you concerned? What are the big uncertainties, the dark clouds? What are you afraid of?

What are the outcomes you want? Think about the time horizon. What do you want for the short term, the medium term, the long term? And what **is** short term, medium and long term to you? Is long term 3 months, a year, 5 years, longer? This is similar to the question "what do you want?" above, but with a focus on the outcome, on what you want this strategy to deliver. The answer does NOT look like "I want a new job where I feel more appreciated and make more money." It has to be much more specific, so that you can focus, achieve and recognize the outcome. The answer looks a bit like a SMART goal (specific, measurable, achievable, realistic and time-bound), but don't get too caught up on the realistic part.

What are the real constraints? No, not what someone else says. Not what you've always told yourself. Challenge your thinking. For each constraint, ask "is it true?" You might discover that it's a block, not a constraint. You just can't think of a way through or around. So here's a trick to think your way through a block. I use it in my coaching practice all the time. When a client says "I don't know" I say "but if you did know, what would you say?" You know what? They almost always answer with something brilliant, because they really do know! So ask yourself, "if this thing were possible, how would I do it?" You're going to winnow the list down to things that really are constraints, not BS beliefs (which is a totally other book, by the way.)

Find your intuition and add it to the mix. There are lots of definitions for intuition. I think intuition is a way of knowing what you know without knowing exactly how you know it. That's a tongue twister. Intuition uses all the information sources you have available to gather data and bypasses the conscious analytical function of your brain to process and reach a conclusion, so that you can completely skip the analysis-paralysis phase. You can trust your intuition. If you've forgotten how, or are slightly skeptical, try it for this part of building your strategy—for getting clarity. Just trust that it is another information source. Or trust me. If you're the kind of person who needs some scientific support before you are willing to try something, Google the Gut/Brain Connection and Intuition. There's all kinds of evidence out there that intuition works, we just don't know exactly *how* it works yet. But birds flew even before we knew how they did it, right?

Okay, now take a break and reflect. You've done a lot of work, so stop and let it sink in. Think about all this. Let it sit for a couple of days. That's the simmering phase. Pay attention to what comes into your world, what crosses your awareness barrier. I believe that you will experience some interesting "coincidences" and get some insights from unexpected places, have some unplanned conversations on the topic that help you tease out some things. Synchronicity. It's the seasoning for the risotto.

After you've come back, reviewed, revised and incorporated the gifts of thoughts, insights and honesty that have come your way answer these last two sets of questions.

Finding your "Why". Why are you craving a career change? Why are you in a career crisis? Why haven't you pursued what you wanted before? Or if you have, why are you in crisis *now*? What's changed? Have *you* changed? Why do you want what you want? Is there something else going on in your world, your life? What are the real reasons behind what's going on? Is it really a career crisis? Again, any answer is fine, as long as it is *your* answer.

Calling, Career or Job? Now that you have done all this thinking about your life, let's look at your career in context, and ask yourself a hard question, and answer honestly. What are you looking for **right now**? Do you just want something that keeps you busy and pays the bills—"just a job"? Have you "paid your dues" and want to focus on another facet of your life? Are you tired of a string of jobs that don't seem to lead anywhere? Do you want a career with growth and challenge? Or does everything seem kind of empty, and you are looking for your purpose, a calling? Whatever the real answer is, it's okay. Really, it's okay if you don't have a calling as a career. If you admit that, you make space to find it somewhere else! You have a whole broad, big life to live. There's lots of room for a calling and purpose! Contrary to popular belief, it doesn't have to be the way you earn your living! You just need to know the answer now, before we go building a strategy for the wrong thing, right? You've spent the metaphorical 55 minutes, so let's not forget this last piece.

These questions are not exhaustive. This isn't the only way to get clarity. It's not the only way to come up with a strategy. It's one way. There are others. If this way doesn't work for you, try something else. There is not one-size-fits-all anything. Pick what works best for you! The most important thing to remember is to think about how you want to resolve your current career crisis in the context of your whole life. You need a strategy before you jump into action, and you need clarity before you build your strategy.

• • •

It's easy to get overwhelmed with all this heavy thinking stuff. Here's a tip: I was listening to a training call with Stella Orange a couple of months ago, and I heard the best description of overwhelm ever. "Overwhelm is a pile of unmade decisions." Isn't that true? I can just see a big pile of tangled, knotted strings. And the only way out is to make one decision at a time. So if you feel overwhelmed at any time, imagine a booming loudspeaker voice that says "step away from the strategy!" Just stop, take a break, and when you come back, pick one thread and make a small decision. It doesn't need to be the biggest, thorniest, most important decision. It could be something very small, like what color socks to wear. Okay, I confess. There have been times when even making that decision could reduce me to tears and an irresistible urge to crawl under the blankets. That just means a longer break. And something fun for a distraction. You know that pile will be there when you come back, but it just might be a bit smaller if you change your perspective.

Making It Real

Let's talk about Emma, from the waiting room. She's the one who is all over the map. She makes good money, but doesn't like what she's doing. But she can't imagine what else she could do. She wants something with more meaning. She desperately wants to find the right career. She has no energy. She doesn't have time for any of the things that she loves, like music or wilderness. And she's a newlywed. And they have been living in sublets for about a year. And she wants babies. She can't figure it out. She feels a huge compulsion to start taking classes so that she can build her skills, she just has no idea what classes to take. If there was ever an example of someone who could use some clarity, it's Emma. Emma is a client of mine. Before working with me, she did a lot of career counseling, taking personality and skills assessments and finding out what fields would be a good fit. Trouble is, the answers always made her want to cry. So we started with a different approach, which was (no surprise here) getting some clarity on what she wants out of the various areas of her life. She doesn't have her dream job just yet, but they've moved into an apartment, they've taken a couple of vacations. She doesn't have her strategy completed yet, but she is enjoying her life while she figures it out. She's calmed down enormously. She no longer lives in a sense of panic. She knows her priorities and has really narrowed down her interests. She's making big strides now.

Making It Yours

I'm not providing more questions here, like I do in other chapters, because, duh, this chapter is all about questions. What I will do is give you a challenge—or an opportunity, if that sounds better.

This is not the time to keep secrets, especially from yourself. Look, you're taking the time to get really clear on what you want for your future—for your life—so that you can create a strategy to get just that. This strategy is NOT about what your parents want for you, or what your Uncle Dan thinks is the best move for you, or the advice from your boss or mentor or anyone else. It's about you. Later on in the process you will take other people's thoughts, feelings and needs into consideration. But they don't drive this step—Clarity—because it's all about you. Full stop.

So the challenge is this: go back and review the questions and see if you've been keeping any secrets. Is there something you've been afraid to admit, even to yourself? For example, is there more to the problem than you included? Maybe there's more going on than just your career? Is there something you want, but you didn't write down because you thought it sounded petty, selfish, insignificant, unflattering or unachievable? Add it anyway. Are you feeling something that might be embarrassing to tell someone else? You don't need to share this stuff with anyone. Are there things that are important to you that aren't on the list because you think it might make you appear different from how you want people to see you? Again, don't share. And don't worry about it—you are a good person. You can be complex! Or shallow. Or whatever, as long as it's you.

I think you get the picture. Go deeper. Be honest. Don't worry about what other people might think if they read your secret diary. If you have to lock it up so that no one reads it—do it. Or put it online with a password. If you share space with someone, don't put this stuff on the wall. But even more importantly, don't rule something out because you don't believe it can happen for you, okay?

You'll have opportunities to dismiss things later. But for now at least, make sure there are no secrets from yourself.

Exercise: Web of Life

One of my favorite exercises is the Web of Life.

You can download it here, along with the rest of the workbook. www.ohsnap-thebook.com/

This is a visual self-assessment tool, a spider diagram, representing the web that is made up when you weave the different areas of your life together. What's important to you, what isn't?

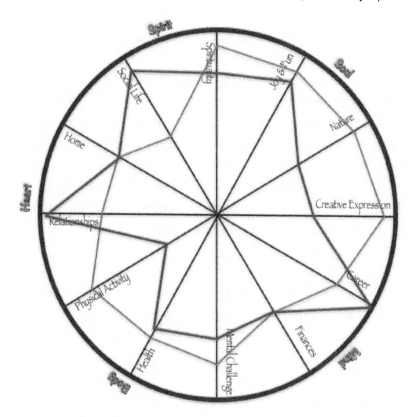

How balanced is your life? How satisfied are you? What areas need more attention?

After you download and print it out, follow these instructions.

1. In your favorite color, place a dot on each line representing how important that area of life is to you. Connect the dots with that color.

2. In a different color, place a dot on each line indicating how satisfied you are with each area, and connect the dots.

Close to the edge is very important/satisfied; close to the center is unimportant/dissatisfied.

Connect the dots to see how balanced your web is, and how aligned your life is with your values.

Look for areas where there are gaps between how important something is to you and how satisfied you are with it. Those areas need some attention. There might be areas where you are giving too much attention to something that really isn't important to you, too.

This exercise will help you with the steps that are coming up. But it also might help prompt you to think of things that you want to add to your answers in this section.

• • •

Here's a really random present, because we talked about risotto so much. I have a short-cut recipe for risotto. There's no short-cut for clarity, so you might as well take this. It works well in bigger batches, too.

1 cup of short grain brown rice (the shorter the better, and it's gotta be brown)
4 cups of water or chicken broth (that's right, twice as much water as normal)
2-3 T Knorr chicken bouillon (sure, you can change brands)
4 T Coconut oil (more if you want)
1 T garlic salt (more if you want)

Bring it all to a boil in a big pot. Stir. Turn way, way down to a low simmer. Some bubbles need to be going on, but not much or it won't get the right texture. Let it cook until the water is fully absorbed. That's gonna be 2–3 hours, but keep an eye on it. Stir every half hour or so.

The magic of the flavor is the combo of the bouillon and the coconut oil. You can add stuff like mushrooms, parsley, or whatever. I've even added lentils and carrots before. I probably won't do that again, but I'll keep experimenting. It's absolutely awesome served with grilled chicken sausages and green salad. Just to be clear.

. . . .
JOT SPOT
. . . .

Oh, did I catch you without some sticky notes??
Jot a quick note here, you can expand later in the workbook!

Chapter 5

STEP 3. CURIOSITY

•••••••••••••••••••

Research and explore your options with curiosity and objectivity

> *The important thing is not to stop questioning. Curiosity has its own reason for existing.*
> *—Albert Einstein*

> *Curiosity will conquer fear even more than bravery will.*
> **—James Stephens**

The goal of this step is to open the doors (to your strategy, to your future) a **lot** wider, so you can fit more things through them. So now you get to go and be curious, to explore. If you're thinking, "that seems like an odd step in creating a strategy. Why does she say to do that?" then I say, "Yay! You're curious!"

I just Googled curiosity, and saw the best quote: "Curiosity makes you smarter." It's an advertising slogan for curiosity.com, a site that offers short learning bites, memes and videos. My favorite title so far is Are Mites Having Sex on Your Face? Awesome. Maybe I won't explore that one.

Does curiosity make you smarter? Sure. Yes. Absolutely. Being curious means your brain is engaged. Following your curiosity teaches you things: how to ask questions, how to ask BETTER questions, how to find answers, and yes, even the answers to the questions. Being smart means being quick-witted or intelligent. Intelligence is not memorizing a lot of things; it is not even knowing a lot of information. Intelligence is the ability to *acquire* and *apply* knowledge. Following our curiosity is how we acquire knowledge; trying things out is how we apply it. So curiosity *does* make you smarter.

How does that apply to creating your strategy? It seems obvious to me, but here it is. You don't want an average strategy. You want a *great* strategy, a smart strategy, one that works for you, one that will help you get what you want. You just spent time getting clear on the problem and the outcome that you want. You'll do a better job if you work out your brain a bit and get smarter. You could do a bunch of Sudoku, I guess, but I don't think that sounds very fun. Certainly there's not much variety there. You can do better.

And another thing. You are not starting out at the beginning (of your life, of your career) so there really aren't any "done for you" templates for the strategy for solving your particular career dilemma. You're actually looking for a very specific thing here—a strategy to get what you want—but it doesn't exist yet. You have to create it, so that means you need to be creative as well as smart.

Curiosity is about exploration, research and inquisitiveness. Think about a curious child—how do they approach life? They touch, taste, smell and look at everything! They ask lots of questions. They try things out.

Scientists, explorers and adventurers are the grown up versions of the curious child. A side note on the science thing: curiosity is not the same thing as analysis, and we certainly don't want you getting caught up in analysis paralysis, okay? Another thing about getting curious is that you need to suspend both disbelief and judgment. You want to be like a research scientist—open minded, objective and not too heavily influenced by assumptions. Sure, you'll reach a conclusion, but AFTER you've done some research and gathered some data. You want to be like an explorer, who has an idea about where they are going, but are wide open to being surprised about what they discover once they get there. And you want to be like an adventurer, who is willing to take a different path to follow the possibility of an adventure.

I have to say something about objectivity here. It's a bit of a myth. We can't be 100% completely and totally objective. We will always have a perspective, a couple of preconceived notions, an answer that we are secretly rooting for the win, or some enlightened self-interest. That's okay. It's nice if we are honest enough to be aware of it, right? You want to be as objective as you can be, noting your biases. But even more important is to do that thing I mentioned earlier—suspend disbelief and judgment.

Stop telling yourself that you can't do something. If you get any hint of these kinds of thoughts: "it's too late for me", "I'm not good enough", "I don't deserve", "that would be selfish" or any variation on these themes, please, please, please just stop! You might think that you are protecting yourself or just being honest, but in reality you are cutting yourself off from a whole lot of potential. Here's a great test: would you say any of this stuff to a young son or daughter or niece or nephew that you love very much? If it's not okay to say to them, it's not okay to say to yourself.

I see one thing over and over with my clients that absolutely appalls me. They are mean. They say horrible things. They are bullies. They have ridiculously unrealistic expectations. The stuff that comes out of their mouths, well, let's just say that there isn't enough soap in the world. Oh, they would never ever think of saying these things to another person—they say them to and about themselves. They punish themselves with constant guilt. They nag and yell at themselves—as if that would do any good! Yeah, yeah, I know. I used to do it, too. It's a cultural norm, I think, for good people to make themselves feel bad. I cannot tell you how different my life became when I stopped yelling at myself. When I acknowledged that I am a good person (yes I'm flawed, but I really am doing my best and trying harder every day to do better) I had so much more energy left to **be** that person. Beating myself up never really accomplished what I wanted to accomplish. I could never yell or nag myself thinner, happier, nicer, smarter, more successful, more generous, funnier or prettier. I could yell myself miserable, though. It was a bit of a gradual process, really. I learned that if I stopped, I felt relieved. And the more I pursued the relief, the more I became who I wanted to be. I was pretty astounded that it was that simple, let me tell you! So if you only take away one thing from this whole book, please let it be that if you stop being a bully to yourself, you will not only *feel* better, you will *be* better. Don't say anything to yourself that you wouldn't say to that young child that you love.

Do you feel like you need to ask it again? "Why do I need to be curious to develop my strategy? It has to be practical." I'll answer you. You have questions, a dilemma or two to solve. I'll give you another Einstein quote. "We cannot solve our problems with the same thinking we used when we created them." If you want to create a strategy that gets you out of your current crisis, you need to think differently as you craft your strategy. Getting curious will make you think differently. By the way, it is a total accident that so many of my quotes come from Albert Einstein. If you believe in accidents, that is. I really wish I had met him. When we figure out how to time travel, I think that's the first place I'm going. Or maybe to the Council of Nicea, to find out what the heck they were thinking, and who was in power, and whether they had any idea of the kind of impact their book would have on the world. But I digress with my curiosity. And that's exactly what I want you to do for a little while.

I guess another way to say it is that if you keep doing what you're doing, you'll get what you got. I thought this was a Twelve Step saying, but it's actually a bit butchered up Henry Ford quote. If you want something different than what you have now—if you want to get out of your career crisis—you are going to have to do something different, think differently, be different.

Okay, back to the assignment. Step out of your comfort zone. Put on your favorite scientist or adventurer or explorer hat and get curious. I talk about this in depth in my book, *Whoops! I Forgot to Achieve My Potential*. I'm not gonna repeat the whole thing here, so let's just say that putting on a hat is like stepping into character. Pretend you are the person who always follows their curiosity and seeks adventure. Act as if and voila, ta-da, presto! That's who you are!

• • •

What are you supposed to be curious about? Ah, finally, a good question! Get curious about the things you discovered in the last step, getting clarity. Maybe you have things to check out in the parking lot—some of those random ideas. What are your options? What do you like or not? Sample. Taste. Touch. Try. Investigate. Try before you buy. Volunteer. Check out events. Talk to people. Brainstorm. Dream. Google search. YouTube. TedTalks. Pull at threads, see where they go. Talk to more people. Check stuff out! I can't tell you exactly what to do, because you have to follow your own interests and curiosity.

Keep this in mind: there is no one-size-fits-all anything. Know that you are figuring out what works for you. Not everything will fit. You'll find that you like some things you weren't expecting to like, and don't really like things that you thought you might. Find your own opinions, don't just follow the experts. You can get their advice, but do your own research, gather your own data, form your own opinions and draw your own conclusions.

Keep what you want, dismiss what you don't want. You might want to revise your answers from the last chapter. Cool. Your strategy will contain better solutions because you were curious. It's okay to revise your answers at any time in this process, because your strategy is a living thing—just like you are!

Once you start this, you may never stop. You might turn into a really curious person (not in a Benjamin Button kind of way). That would be awesome, and probably way more effective at keeping your memory sharp than all those puzzles. And way more fun, too. That doesn't mean you can't ever get started on the next step. You'll know when you're ready. It doesn't have to take months or years or even weeks. Well, maybe a couple of weeks. It takes what it takes. You can actually do the next step while you're exploring. The two go together well.

Making It Real

So let's talk about Lisa, the first person we met in the waiting room. There are a lot of things going on with Lisa. She works ridiculous hours. Her life is one big stress-fest and her body doesn't like it. Neither does she, but she doesn't know how to get out of it. No idea. In fact, saying things like "no, I'm not going to work on Saturday" doesn't enter her mind as a possibility. Lisa came to me thinking that she wanted to find a different job that didn't take so much out of her. While working with her, I think the phrase I heard the most was, "that never even occurred to me." It's certainly the most powerful thing she has said, because it shows how disconnected she is from her imagination and curiosity. She wanted out, but couldn't even imagine how to do it, or what else she could do.

Lisa was also one of the worst self-bullies I have ever met. It just about broke my heart, because she is also one of the most genuinely warm and caring people I have ever met. When Lisa started to stop being a bully—yes, it took a while because it was such an ingrained habit—she began to see possibilities. She opened up her curiosity, started dreaming and checking things out. Based on what she discovered, she decided to add things in to her life, and used those to begin to crowd out work. She checked out several possible career changes, and ultimately decided that she wanted to retire a few years early, and spend more time with family, giving back and volunteering. Those were her priorities. She had worked hard enough, and had enough money set aside to be able to do that—it had just never occurred to her as a possibility. Her strategy is all around how to leave her job and create her new life within the next year. It's a very different outcome than she originally thought she could have, but it's the one she wants.

Making It Yours

You might be having a little trouble deciding just what you want to be curious about. I find that once you have a few things on a "list" there's a kind of momentum that happens and you find more and more things. The list can be things about life, work, career, hobby, etc. So make a list, and stick pretty much to it. You can easily go chasing gophers down rabbit holes, which might be fun, but not the most productive use of your time. But sometimes you are actually chasing a valuable lead, so if you digress, check in to see if you're still kind of on track. It's a delicate balance between pulling threads and chasing gophers.

Here are some starter questions to help you refine your list:

1. When I look at the gaps from the Web of Life exercise, what things jump out at me as possible ways to bridge the gap? Put them on your list. (For example, you might have a gap in creative expression, and you think that pottery or poetry might be something you could try to fill it.)

2. What kind of things did I put in the parking lot? Is there anything that I feel compelled to explore right now?

3. What kinds of things did I discover in the last step when I went back looking for secrets? Like, did I secretly always want to be a private detective?

4. What did I think about doing when I was a little kid?

5. What do I think about in my spare time? What kinds of questions do I ask? Is there a theme, a field, a career opportunity, a hobby or something like that to explore here?

6. What do I do in my spare time, for fun or challenge? Explore how that might be related to a career, or elements incorporated in a career.

7. If anything were possible, what would I like to do? Maybe there is a real reason why you can't do it, but look around the edges for related possibilities.

8. Use your imagination and intuition—what comes to you (even if it seems random) to explore.

9. What's your heart's desire?

Exercise

This space is intentionally left blank (because this step is made up of a whole bunch of exercises!)

● ● ● ● ● ● ● ● ● ●
JOT SPOT
● ● ● ● ● ● ● ● ●

Oh, did I catch you without some sticky notes??
Jot a quick note here, you can expand later in the workbook!

Chapter 6

STEP 4. CHALLENGE

· · · · · · · · · · · · · · · · · ·

Call out your assumptions and challenge them

"Assumptions are dangerous things to make, and like all dangerous things to make—bombs, for instance, or strawberry shortcake—if you make even the tiniest mistake you can find yourself in terrible trouble. Making assumptions simply means believing things are a certain way with little or no evidence that shows you are correct, and you can see at once how this can lead to terrible trouble. For instance, one morning you might wake up and make the assumption that your bed was in the same place that it always was, even though you would have no real evidence that this was so. But when you got out of your bed, you might discover that it had floated out to sea, and now you would be in terrible trouble all because of the incorrect assumption that you'd made. You can see that it is better not to make too many assumptions, particularly in the morning."

—**Lemony Snicket**, The Austere Academy

I t's time to build on the mindset of the previous step. I said that the two steps go together well, and that's because they both take a really open mind. This step is about separating limiting beliefs from true constraints.

Half of the time we don't even know that our assumptions are assumptions. We think they are facts, truth, reality. For example, I just said half of the time. I don't know if it's really half of the time—maybe it's 23% of the time. Half the time we take things at face value, without questioning whether they are really true or not. See, I just did it again. It doesn't really matter in this case, it doesn't have to be 100% accurate, because I'm just using the illustration to make a point—that we are often unaware that we are making assumptions. But the ideas and beliefs that we base big life decisions on—those things had better be true!

It's time to do a little CYA (that's corporate speak for "cover your *ss"), because you know what they say about assuming, right? The whole ass-u-me thing? Well, in this case, building your strategy by assuming means that you are building it on a premise **without proof that it is even true!** You could be building your strategy on a solid foundation or something really shaky—like a House of Cards episode!

Call out your assumptions. First, you want to **identify** your assumptions so that you know what they are—name them. Awareness is always the most powerful thing you can do to solve a problem. More accurately stated, nothing happens without awareness—except accidents. With all the work you've put in so far, you don't want your strategy to be an accident, right? So you need to lay out your assumptions. The exercise at the end of this chapter will help you find 'em.

Challenge your assumptions. Now that you've identified them, are they true? Really? Challenge your thinking. Are you basing your entire strategy, career, maybe even your success on an assumption that is wrong? Tap into the skills you developed in the last chapter. Take the time to do a little research to make sure that your assumptions really are true. Maybe they were at one time, but aren't anymore. The world changes pretty quickly these days! For example, you may be assuming that you must have a specialist degree to get a promotion you want, but is that true? Do you have comparable experience that an employer might value just as highly? You don't have to check every single thing, but certainly check the foundational assumptions!

Creatively address your assumptions. This is really the most important part of this step, because it begins the process of creative problem solving. Start with some of your limiting assumptions. So even if something is true, does it have to be? Are you accepting a constraint that doesn't have to be there? Can you see any way around this assumption? Use the "what if I did know?" trick from Step 2 to see what you might come up with as a solution! This is another great opportunity to enlist your trusted advisors. Ask them if there is a solution that you might not be seeing right now. Here's a bonus: don't be surprised if you get super inspired and come up with new and awesome ideas. That's what happens when you engage your creativity with an open mind.

If you are left with anything at this stage—assumptions that you haven't been able to dismiss, in fact that you've confirmed—you're going to be left with a list of truths. Some of those might be constraints. Check them one more time, to make sure they aren't actually limiting beliefs. My second book is all about finding and removing outdated and limiting beliefs. They can be hard to find, because you've lived with them for so long that you can't even see them anymore, just like that stain on the rug from that party eight years ago. There are some indicators that you might have a limiting belief. You can read this like you would one of those old "you might be a redneck" jokes. You might have a limiting belief if

- You feel jealous of what other people are able to do.
- You feel sad, miserable, angry or any other really intense emotion.
- You feel like the rules apply differently to you than others.
- Other people do things that don't even occur to you.
- You've got a lot of guilt around the topic.

There are more, but you get the gist—look for something that just doesn't fit. Once you've identified the limiting beliefs, you can choose to do something about them. Namely, choose not to believe them anymore, not think those thoughts and not have them drive your behavior. Yeah, that sounds really simple. I know that it isn't exactly simple, but let's not get too far off topic. We'll talk about it a bit more in Chapter 11.

For now, once you've separated out the limiting beliefs, you have your list of true constraints. It's important to know the difference. Set them aside for now, you'll use them when we craft and test your strategy. Hopefully, that won't be first thing in the morning.

Making It Real

Louisa is the woman in the waiting room who was wearing running gear, the one who had taken several years "off" raising her special needs child and is now returning to the work force. She was jealous of the millennial mindset. She wondered if it's too late for her. She didn't really think that she had any current skills—especially the tech skills that even infants seem to be born with these days. I'm sure you can see that Louisa was making a lot of assumptions here. Some things might be true, like she might want to spend some time becoming a bit more comfortable with technology, but the amount of time she needs to invest depends upon what career she decides to pursue. But most of her assumptions were just holding her back from even exploring possibilities, and adding to her worry and stress. As of today, she's done a great job separating out her assumptions and updating her limiting beliefs. She's currently coming up with creative ways to use her "non-traditional" experience to her advantage, rather than assuming that it will keep her from finding fulfilling work.

Making It Yours

- What are your assumptions? Can you find them? Go back through your work so far and look for the "unspoken rules" that you applied.

- Are any of them silly? Can you look at them light-heartedly, like Lemony Snicket?

- When you get to a negative assumption, a limiting assumption, go try to find an example of someone who proves that it isn't true. Then another. Try to find as much evidence as you can that it isn't true!

- Find someone that you trust, that supports you, someone who believes in you and thinks that you can do whatever you set your mind to do, and tell them your story and your assumptions. Ask them to poke holes in your assumptions.

- When you get to your final list of constraints, are there any that really make you mad, that make you want to rebel? Ask that same person to help you creatively think your way around them. What if they weren't true? What if there was some way…what would it look like?

Exercise: How to find assumptions

The thing is, they can be hard to find. They hide in plain sight. Here are a few tricks for finding assumptions.

1. Look for the most obvious things first, the things that sound simplistic, naive or even dumb.
2. Look for "common knowledge" or "they say" or the like.
3. Look for black and white thinking on your part, where you see only yes or no, limited options, etc.
4. Look for ideas that masquerade as facts, such as "X job doesn't pay enough for me to make a living" or "there's no room for someone with my skills", etc.
5. Take a critical thinking approach. Lay out your logic, and look for gaps or jumps in your thinking.
6. Look for exaggerations. Half the time...
7. Look for emotionally charged conclusions.
8. Give extra focus to the assumptions that are limiting or constraining. Sure, you want to look for the ones that seem overly optimistic, too, but you're probably not going too far down that trail right now. Still, flesh them out, too.
9. Talk to someone you respect who has a different perspective than you have, lay out your thinking and ask them to point out where they don't "jump" to the same conclusion you do.

Aye, matey, thar be assumptions!

• • • • • • • • • •

JOT SPOT

• • • • • • • • •

Oh, did I catch you without some sticky notes??
Jot a quick note here, you can expand later in the workbook!

Chapter 7

STEP 5. CHOOSE

• • • • • • • • • • • • • • • • •

Make Choices Based on *Your* Priorities

*One day Mischa Elman and his wife were leaving Carnegie Hall
by the backstage door. Two tourists approached and noticing
that he was carrying his violin case, asked "How do you get to
Carnegie Hall?"*

"Practice, practice, practice," Mischa replied.

—the story according to the Carnegie Hall website

O kay, here we are. It's just about time to make some decisions.
We've both been avoiding this. I've been procrastinating just
a little on writing this chapter, so yeah, both of us! I did mention,
way back in the chapter on leadership skills, that you were going
to need the ability to make difficult decisions. And that's what's
coming up next.

But before you start in being all decisive, and take-chargy in the old-school stereotype, let me make the announcement that this chapter is about choices, not decisions. It might seem like semantics, but it's really not. Decision making is primarily an ability to effectively analyze options, potential outcomes, risks and mitigation strategies, and then follow up with the leadership skill of picking the best option and sticking to it. Choosing, however, is a super power.

Wait, what are superpowers? Aren't they the stuff of fictional characters, who mostly wear leotard suits with big letters and a shiny cape? That's one definition, but it's not the only one. In my book (and this is my book) superpowers are human qualities and abilities that have been honed and developed to *empower* us to make our world and our lives better by becoming the highest and best version of ourselves. Superpowers aren't for the faint of heart, and they aren't for everyone, but they are *possible* for everyone. Everyone who wants to cultivate their superpowers doesn't have to pick the same powers—we are unique, after all—but Choice (with a capital "C") is pretty much foundational.

Choice and power are intimately related. I'm not talking about world-domination-type power, or political power, or power over other people. I'm talking about personal power. Filling up your skin with confidence, competence, strength, purpose, authenticity and commitment. Personal power feels good. It feels strong, in control, energized, and...well, powerful! Feeling powerless is the worst. It sucks. It feels like we're trapped, don't matter, have no say, options or choice in life, and it totally saps our energy. Ironically, it is when we are powerless that we have to muster everything we have in order to be strong enough to get through! That's exactly what being in crisis is—feeling powerless. You are developing a strategy to take your power back, to be able to choose what will make your life and your career right for you.

Why don't we make choices? We all know the person who goes through life making as few choices as possible. They say "You pick, I can't" when asked where they want to go for dinner. They don't choose anything. Why? Who knows. They don't! Maybe they are caught up in being a people-pleaser, and don't want the responsibility of making a choice that someone else doesn't like, or don't want to seem controlling. Maybe they want to keep their options open. Maybe they can't commit. Making real choices takes practice. Sometimes we're out of practice, or stuck, or lost, or just kinda forgot all about our power because life has happened (and we let it happen). Maybe that even described you at some point—but not anymore, because you are going to get really good at making choices.

Having lots of options will not make you happier with your choice. Talk about synchronicity. I just read today, about an article that reminded me of this fact. It referred to a study in 2002 about consumer jam choices, and how too many choices actually prevented people from making a decision! I totally get that! A few years ago, I had a bunch of people come over from Australia to California to work on a project. One of the first things they noticed was how much variety we have in the grocery store. They were completely overwhelmed at first, and then they laughed. The plethora of options didn't make shopping (choosing) easier or better, and it certainly didn't make them happier to know that they had chosen the very best toilet paper out of all 12 brands!

You don't need to be full of choices. I worked with a "leader" who would talk about making "choiceful decisions". It drove me nuts. She meant to say that we should make careful, thoughtful and intentional decisions—that we should inject the elements of choice into our decisions! Unfortunately, she was misusing the word, because "choiceful" means pretty much the opposite. It means having lots of options from which to choose, or being fickle with your choices. Too bad, really. I like what she intended to say!

Not making a choice is a choice. Delaying or avoiding making a choice is really handing over the power to someone else or to chance. Making a choice isn't a race. You don't need to hurry every choice; some take a little time to fully mature. You might want to wait for some signs or further information, or until you're ready. But you want to learn to find the balance, wait long enough but not too long, to know when to pick the fruit for perfect ripeness. But don't get carried away with the waiting thing. There comes a point when nothing of value is being added to the process, and the fruit will just fall to the ground and rot. The choice will have been made for you.

Making a choice doesn't cut off your options. In fact, the opposite is true: the more choices you make, the more options seem to open up. Your brain loves to choose between two options, that seems to be the easiest, because it just has to compare the two things—which one is better. Sometimes too many options can feel overwhelming. But doesn't it always seem to happen that as soon as you make a choice, another option magically appears? It's like the Murphy's Law of Choice.

You don't even have to have options to make a choice. Wait, what? How can that be true? But it is! You might only have one thing that you can really do, one direction to go. But there is a huge difference between just doing it and fully choosing to do it. You can make a choice, even if you only have one option. Perhaps there is something difficult in your path. You can just slog through, let the momentum of the situation take over. Or you can make choices about how you're going to get through to the other side. You can choose what your attitude will be, what your awareness will be, how you will present to the world. You can choose to be open to opportunities along the way.

So how do you cultivate this superpower?

Try different ways of making choices. I suggest you try a variety of techniques, but start on small things at first—like what to order off of a menu, or what to wear, or something of similar size and magnitude! Whatever you do, avoid the agony! Try choosing from fewer options—choosing between two is a pretty good number. Forget the pro/con lists for a while, try choosing what you really want. Try following your emotions. Try picking what feels good, or what feels "lighter". Try using your body to make choices—muscle testing (yes = strength), as a pendulum (you lean towards what you want), or follow your gut (literally, how does your stomach feel). Practice using your intuition. Meditate. Journal. Practice saying "I choose this" out loud, and try to evoke a sense of conviction, of commitment, because that's a strength building workout!

Practice making choices. Practice, practice, practice. Practice some more. Keep going until you feel like you're good at it, until it's just second nature. Keep practicing until you're a choice making virtuoso, ready for Carnegie Hall.

Amp it up. The very act of choosing creates an intention. Choice is commitment. When you choose to do something, you bring the full power of your choice and conviction and your best—and powerful—self to it. You can make an intellectual decision, and don't need to have much conviction behind it. It's the logical choice. But it can seem a lot like settling—and how far from powerful does that feel? But making a choice is different. Choosing combines the deliberation of a decision with the intention to carry through, to make something happen, maybe even to make magic happen!

• • •

Power is a pretty relevant topic these days. So many people feel the repercussions of the lack of power over their lives. Not everyone reacts the same, so there is anger and division as well as cooperation and compassion. It's a really difficult time, and many of us feel some mix of guilt, futility and responsibility. Maybe you are wondering if you are being just a bit selfish worrying about your own power and superpowers when there are others who "need it more". I want to tell you that in reality, there isn't a limited supply of empowerment. What you have does not need to take away from anyone else's, and someone does not need to be powerless for you to be empowered. That's a myth, just like the idea that happiness is in limited supply—that your happiness comes at a cost to someone else. It's not true, so we can stop behaving as if it is. You can actually be twice as effective (hint: superpower). You can be an example, which has a ripple effect, **and** you can actually do things that make a difference. It's actually much easier to do good things when you feel empowered, rather than desperate and trapped, right?

Making It Real

Let's look at Paul's situation. He had a heart attack one autumn, several years ago. I know, back in the waiting room his heart attack was just last year. That was to make it current, but if I stuck with that timing, you wouldn't know the rest of the story! Anyway, both his doctor and his partner told him that he needed to give up his high-powered, all consuming and high stress corporate job. They told him he had no choice. Paul realized that it wasn't true—he did have a choice. He could choose to stay, but it really wasn't in his best interest. They spent some time getting clear on their priorities, individually and as a couple. It became clear that anything else he would actually choose to do, based on his new priorities, wouldn't pay the big money, and it would mean some big lifestyle changes. Together, they chose to make those changes. They bought a historic building and turned it into a bed & breakfast inn. They built a very cozy and fulfilling life. That option would not have popped up on their radar if he hadn't had a health induced career crisis. Paul didn't accept that he had no choice. He very intentionally took the choice into his own hands, and created a dream life.

Making It Yours

We all know that a single choice can change the direction of our life. That's easy to see looking in the rear view mirror. But how do we see it in real-time? We don't see it; we feel it. We practice making choices until we are so good at it that making choices becomes part of who we are. Follow some of these experiments, and write about what you discover.

What do you know about your own process for decisions and choices? How much input do you get from other people? What do you do with it? Do you trust yourself? How do you make an intellectual choice? What tools do you use, if any? What about emotional choices? Financial choices? Health choices? Other kinds of choices? Are there certain kinds where you rely heavily on the expertise of others, and if so, how do you use their input?

Try using some or all of the different ways to make choices—add your own ideas. How do they feel? What are the results? How well do you think each method works for you? Is there a "customized combination" that would be even more powerful for you?

Pick something that you need to decide. Go through some of the standard decision making processes to see where you would land intellectually. Now go through some of the processes for choosing that you liked from above. Where do you land? Is it the same? Different? How confident do you feel in each scenario? And again, is there a potential combination of decision and choice that might be especially effective for you, and that you would feel really confident using?

What are some of the choices that you've made that changed the direction of your life?

Are there any characteristics in common? Were they about the same facet of your life? Were they easy or hard? How did you make them? Did you know at the time how important that choice was going to be? Would you make a different choice today?

Exercise: Guided Visualization

An audio file of this visualization is included in the workbook.

Try adding a visualization to increase the power of your choice and your intention. A visualization is a virtual experience. You can use your imagination to visualize the pictures and the experience inside your mind's eye. Your brain doesn't really know the difference between the virtual experience and a "real" experience, so you get the benefits.

Sit in a comfortable chair, with your feet planted firmly on the floor. Close your eyes. Take a few breaths until you feel relaxed and peaceful. Go inside. Visualize your choice as a ball of pale blue light.

Now tap into the energy of how much you want this choice, how much you want it to be successful. It's okay if you have to create that energy—you do that by feeling how much hope you have about the results and how much good this choice can bring. This energy is your desire. Visualize it as pink lightning, and as you add it to your ball it grows and takes on a violet hue.

Next, add in the energy that comes from what you dream as it takes its place, the creative space for new opportunities that you open up by making this choice. Visualize that energy and space as pale turquoise lightning and add it to the growing ball.

From deeper inside you, find the energy in you that makes commitments, that makes things happen, that attracts what you want to you. Visualize a flow of that golden energy joining the ball. You can feel the power of this ball, which is reflecting tumbling rainbows of color.

Take this ball, now, and place it in your heart space. It's your living intention. As you move into the actions inspired by this choice, the luminosity of all these energies will light your way.

JOT SPOT

Oh, did I catch you without some sticky notes??
Jot a quick note here, you can expand later in the workbook!

Chapter 8

STEP 6. CRAFT

. . . .

Make Choices Based on *Your* Priorities

"Words are things. You must be careful, careful about calling people out of their names, using racial pejoratives and sexual pejoratives and all that ignorance. Don't do that. Someday we'll be able to measure the power of words. I think they are things. They get on the walls. They get in your wallpaper. They get in your rugs, in your upholstery, and your clothes, and finally into you."
—Maya Angelou

Get out your Sticky notes and your colored pencils or markers. It's time to start pulling your strategy together. You've done the ground work: you've taken the lead, you've sought clarity, you've explored with curiosity, you've challenged your assumptions and you've made choices. So let's go craft! On your mark, get set, be creative. Yeah, that works, right? Hey, if it does work, if you know how you want to draft and craft your strategy, go for it. I'm totally serious. If you know how you want to do it, you will do a better job than you will by following my recommendation, because it will be 100% yours—and that's the most important thing.

But if you don't know how to get started, relax. I'm not going to leave you stranded. In a moment we'll get into specific instructions, and even some visual templates to help you be creative and structured at the same time! But first, I just have to cover a few points.

1. Your strategy is not a plan. I know I'm repeating myself, but it's important. Your strategy defines what you want at a deep enough level to be your guiding star. Your plan tells you what steps you need to take to achieve your strategy. You will build your plan from your strategy. Your plan will probably change a bit as life happens, as you react to reality and as you learn what works and doesn't work. Okay? So your strategy will not contain anything that sounds like an action item. By the way, your plan will be better for this. In items 2 & 3 below, you'll get the gift of something I call "inspired action".

2. Words matter. I love the quote by Maya Angelou at the top of this chapter so much. "Someday we'll be able to measure the power of words." Until then, we need to take it on faith that words have enormous power, respect that power and, I believe, treat them with the same awe, caution and respect that we treat other forces of nature—like the

ocean or the wind. So be really, really particular about the words that you choose to include in your strategy. Words carry energy, words create energy. These words will inspire you to specific actions. These words will attract your attention to key individuals, pieces of information, and opportunities. The wrong words can keep you blind to those possibilities. Words matter.

3. Look for signs. This is building on the idea that your attention will be attracted to things that fit into your vision and your strategy. You'll see a whole lot more things that are relevant to you "all of a sudden." Seriously, have you ever bought a car, and then noticed how many of that exact same car you see on the road? Or learn a new word, and suddenly hear it used three times in two days? Let me extend the thought…have you ever—no, how many times have you needed to know something, needed inspiration or had the start of a really important idea and then something crosses your path that is exactly what you needed? When you are open to it, it happens all the time. I've learned to recognize these synchronicities as signs, and I follow them. I don't just take them on blindly, but I recognize that they are exactly what I need right now, and I don't waste time worrying about whether or not they really are for me. I can get as much out of encountering an idea that I don't agree with as one that supports what I think, because it can help me to hone my own thinking. Why does this happen? I don't really care. I think there might be a scientific explanation that has to do with energy, thoughts and attraction. And there's definitely a

lot of filtering of irrelevant input going on in our brain. Like how we see our nose all the time, but we don't *notice* it? That's the brain doing it's filtering thing. When you intentionally change your definition of relevant, the brain updates its filters!

4. Keep it simple. There are no bonus points for complexity. You're not out to impress anyone, not even yourself. It's better for your strategy to be true than brilliant. There are all kinds of factors we could add in to make sure it's comprehensive. I had to really work to keep extraneous stuff out. When you are lost, you just want simple directions. You don't need a quadratic equation. When you want to be focused, you really don't need distractions. Keep it simple so that you can remember it, and so that your strategy can really be useful to you when you make decisions and decide actions.

5. Oh yeah, one more major thing. We are going to start by crafting your **Life** Strategy. Surely you know why by now. Then we'll focus on your Career Strategy, because it needs to support and enable your Life Strategy. So don't faint when we don't even talk directly about career in the first few steps, okay?

Okay, I think we are ready to begin. If you haven't done it already, go to my website here www.OhSnap-theBook.com/ and download the workbook now. The workbook gives you two options. If you are a visual person, there is a graphical template. If you're better with words, there's a writing template. Print out the version of the strategy template that you want to use. Then pull out the work that you've done so far, you'll use it for reference.

You are going to distill down the important things from the previous steps, and include them in your strategy. Start with Step 1—Courage. You are the owner of your life and your strategy, so invoke the leadership attributes from step 1 that are the most important to you at this point in your life and going forward. Keep them in mind as you make the decisions you need to make.

Many of the elements of your strategy will come directly from your work in Step 2—Clarity. All of your work is good work and will be useful going forward, and you aren't throwing it away… but you will choose what things to extract and include in your strategy. They will be the most important things, the essence of what you want and how you want to be. I don't recommend going straight to the template and trying to fill it in. That will likely lead you to a big pile of overwhelm. I do suggest claiming a wall as your strategy wall, writing down all your potential answers on sticky notes and sticking them up there. Then you can winnow and arrange and add more and rearrange—over and over—until you like what has emerged.

Once that happens, you can fill in the templates. I mentioned before that I'd give you a little more info on my theories around the psychology of sticky notes, and now is the time. Yes, it's a little bit of a digression, but maybe it will convince you to try my way instead of going straight to the template.

- First, stickies come in colors. They aren't what you usually write on (unless you're like me!) Most of them don't have lines. All of these things help you tap into the more creative part of your brain. You are automatically in brainstorming mode.
- Stickies are little. They force you to identify the essence of your idea and a few representational words. You don't

really get to waste a lot of time word-smithing. You move faster, almost as fast as you can think, so you don't lose very many ideas.

- Stickies are not designed to be permanent. This facilitates many wonderful things. Since they aren't permanent, they don't need to be perfect, and your inner critic can take a break. You can change your mind, you don't need to commit to an idea, you can play with it. Your imagination is freed up.

- Stickies are moveable. You can rearrange, prioritize, be flexible. You don't need to decide the structure (or format) before you start. You can go with the flow and see what emerges—it doesn't have to be a list or a paragraph. It's easier to compare one idea to another, to merge things that are related, and to ultimately get rid of things that don't add value.

- Your end result is more organic, more adaptable, cleaner, richer and more diverse than just sitting down in front of a blank sheet of paper. So I guess I could summarize by saying that using sticky notes fosters a sustainable mind-garden. And they're recyclable!

Hopefully you are now convinced that this is the way to go. So grab your pack(s) of stickies and a marker and get ready to do some distillation work. You're going to work with stickies, adding, arranging and rearranging until you distill down to the elements that will go in your strategy. You'll lay them out in a particular order—I'll give you instructions. You'll need two areas of wall space, one for your workspace and one for your final answers. Here's the layout for the "final answers" workspace:

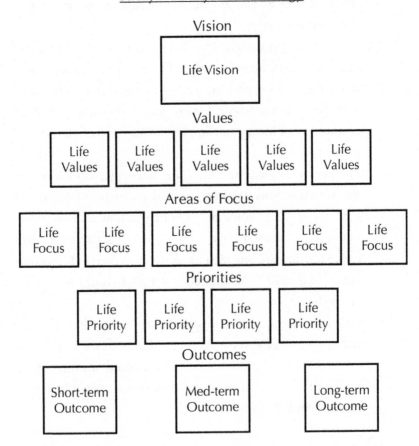

Sticky-note Layout for Strategy

Once you have all of your answers and have completed the layout, you can move them into a final strategy document. Ooooh, that all sounds so official, doesn't it? In the workbook, I've included a few templates. You don't need to do all of them, pick the one that you like. For the visual people, there are a couple of visual templates, the standard "house and pillars" and a cartoony roadmap, but of course you can draw your own if you're so inspired. For the verbal people, there's a document type template. You might want to try doing the document and then a visual template, just for fun.

There are five elements to your strategy. They are your vision, priorities, values, areas of focus and outcomes, but not necessarily in that order. As I mentioned many times earlier on, we are going to focus on your life strategy first. We'll get to the elements of your career strategy a bit later. They'll be the same elements, but they will be supporting the elements of your life strategy.

Outcomes. Let's start with something easy. Hah! These are some of your life goals, right? It's not exactly a roadmap, (that's your plan) but it certainly is context. So look through your clarity work again, and pull out the outcomes you want. Yes, on stickies! Of course! Now give them a relationship to each other in these time frames: short, medium, and long term. Another way to ask this is: What do I want to have as my reality in the short term? Medium term? etc. If you've got lots of desired outcomes, you're gonna have to make a choice. You can't keep "wishing for more wishes" by sticking a bunch of "ands" in between outcomes. To be clear, I'm not saying you can't have it all, or you have to give up wanting lots of things. For the purposes of your strategy, however, you do have to put on your super suit and choose what are the most important outcomes and when do you want them. What if you have conflicting outcomes? Well, you have to resolve the conflict!!! How? By choosing. No way around it. For example, say you want to live in a mansion and you want to lead a simple life? You are going to have to choose the one that is most important. (By the way, that might seem like an irreconcilable conflict—until you choose one as the guiding principle, the most important. Then your brain can relax and start working creatively on how to solve the problem of bringing both together. It's amazing how that works!)

Once you have the outcomes you want in the time frames you want them, get a little more specific. What does short term mean to you, in the context of your life strategy? 6 weeks? 3 months? 1 year? Answer for each one. You don't set that date range first, because your brain would go about trying to answer the question: "what can I realistically get done in 3 months?" That's a very different question than "what do I want in the short term?" Right? It can't help it. Its job is to solve the problem we put in front of it—that's why it's the brains of the outfit.

These outcomes, and the timeframes *you* assign, go at the very bottom of your "final answers" workspace. You are going to leave some blank space between them, enough for some supporting career outcomes...but that comes later.

Priorities. Next, you're going to identify what's important. Review your work on clarity, and pull out your priorities. Write them on stickies and play with them in your workspace until you have a set of 3 or 4 that really represent the top priorities in your life. If you have a ton of priorities and have difficulty picking your top 3, arrange them randomly in a vertical line and work through them, two at a time, like you would a tournament bracket. Is this one more or less important to me than that one? Visually move it forward. Keep going until they've all competed and you have your winners. See? A ranking emerges! Take the top 3 or 4 stickies as your priorities. These become the foundation, so you are going to lay them out at the bottom, just above the outcomes.

Values. It's easy to confuse values with priorities. Values are also important to you, but they have to do with what you ethically and morally hold dear to you. Values determine how you want to behave, how you want the experience to be and how you want to feel. We didn't do an exercise in Clarity to have you define your values. No, I didn't forget to ask you to do it. The timing wasn't right. I wanted them to be in context. I didn't want you to go to the Big List of Values and circle your top 25. Yeah, that's a thing and sometimes it's useful. But I bet your list would be a little different, not because you're fickle and you don't have values. It's that context thing again. So, knowing that you are talking about your Life Strategy, and you've identified your top priorities and outcomes, now identify your values: the way you live your life, how you walk when you walk your talk about your life strategy. Yep, list them all and whittle the list down, compare, contrast, prioritize. That's all another way to say "Choose" your top 5.

Focus Areas. There are lots of things in life that interest you, lots of things that you want to explore, I know. But you can't focus on everything, or else you lose focus. Let me segue into a metaphor of designing a house. You've got a fixed amount of space to build in, so when you design your floor plan, you have to figure out what kinds of rooms you want in your home. These are your areas of focus, what's important enough in your life to actually include in your house. Some things won't make the cut, but that doesn't mean you won't ever experience them. You'll just have to go outside your home to get to them. Some things you might want in your life, but only on occasion.

So you have to pick a reasonable number of things to focus on, find the balance that works for you. Why? Well, too few rooms might cause you to blur some things together. A bathdiningroom isn't an awesome combination, neither is a kitchoffice, or gymnbedroom. Too many rooms mean that the ones that really need more space will have to sacrifice to accommodate getting all the others in. So figure out what makes sense to you. Okay, that's enough with the house metaphor.

Look through all of the work you did in the past few chapters, look for patterns and pick out the things that are important to you.

You can use the Web of Life Assessment for high level categories. Do the whole sticky note thing to come up with a reasonable number of rooms. What's reasonable? Let's say 4—8. I gave you room for 6 as a placeholder.

Vision statement. And now you get to put the cherry on top. Your vision statement is the summary of all your "whats" and their "whys". There is a ton of conventional wisdom about how to write a good vision statement, especially in a business context. It doesn't all agree. A lot of it is outward facing, describing who the business or organization is so that the public can understand. Sometimes it's called the elevator pitch. Sometimes it's a PR statement. That doesn't really matter here. This is not outward-facing, it's for you.

Your vision statement should reflect your dream, what you believe is ideal *for you in your life.* It should provide you with enough direction to remind you of your dream, motivate you when you need motivation, and help you to identify the right direction. When you have to make an important decision, it should have enough depth to be the deciding factor. It doesn't have to be all inclusive and wordy, with provisions for every possibility. It's not a legal document—it's your guiding star.

It's not going to fit on a small sticky note in reasonably sized handwriting, so you can summarize on a bigger piece of paper. Oh, and you have to love, love, love it. So it might take a couple of revisions. You can play with stickies, using them like the refrigerator magnet poetry games that used to be so popular!

Once you get all of these pieces right (in your opinion, not mine) put them into your word-based template or one of the pictures, or both if you feel the inclination. You might want to use pencil, in case you want to adjust something slightly. That's your life strategy document. It's a living document, so it is okay to change and update if you want.

• • •

Now if you are looking at the layout, you will see that there are still some blank spots. These are placeholders, reserved for the elements of your career strategy. See how they are integrated into your life strategy, part of the whole picture? That's by accident, not design. Ha, just checking to see if you were still with me. It's by design, not accident. For preparation you can look at the career related information you came up with in the previous chapters. You can also do the "what I want in a job" exercise from the workbook, if you want to spend some time getting your head into the specifics.

• • •

Let's continue on, tightening the focus to the arena of career. Now that you're familiar with this process, it should be easier. Continue with the sticky note methodology, which I know you get by now, so I'm not going to repeat the instructions. I'll just provide some tighter questions, to help focus on career and how it supports your life strategy.

It's really important that you remember that bit about supporting your life strategy. It's also important to be honest. And to resolve conflicts. And choose. And all that stuff. You just might learn something really important by looking at your career this way. For example, title and growth and responsibility might have been really important to you in the past, when you looked at it solely through the lens of career and inherent ambition. But when you take your life strategy into consideration, salary, location and fulfilling work may emerge as important. That's a conflict, all right, and it just might be at the root of your whole work/life balance crisis. You learned something big—that your work priorities and your life priorities have been in conflict. Now you have to choose which is more important, and craft your work priorities appropriately. And remember, that gets the brain working to resolve the conflict, a task you hadn't really given it before, so you may come up with a solution you hadn't seen before. That's a real life example from one of my clients, by the way. It might seem super obvious to you, but that's because you aren't in the middle of it. It was incredibly freeing to her—and she did come up with a balanced solution! Who knows what you might learn for yourself!

Start with outcomes, just like you did with life. What career related outcomes do you want, in order to support the outcomes you want in your life. That's the first way to look at it, but it is also okay to have some outcomes that support what you want out of a career, as long as they don't conflict with life outcomes. That kind of conflict leads to career crisis, remember? If it seems like a conflict, see if you can creatively solve the conflict. If not (at least for now) then make a choice.

Next, do the priorities. What are the priorities for your career? How do they support your life strategy? If there's a conflict, make a choice. It's okay to adapt, just don't agonize! Choose your top 3 priorities.

Now identify your values. This might end up being one of the areas where you discover a previously existing condition. You might have felt like two separate people—you at work, and you the rest of the time, each having their own distinct values and behaviors. That's really hard to do, and not at all necessary. I think it's at the core of a lot of career crises, especially the ones that feel like mid-life crises, disconnected from purpose, integrity and expression. You can start to do something about it here, by aligning your career values to your life values. It doesn't necessarily mean you have to change *what* you do. You can change *how* you do it—how you behave, how you treat people, what you say, etc.

Sometimes just the realization that there's a schism helps start the alignment process. I don't mean to imply that you've been obtuse or not self-aware. I just suggest changing perspective to get a fresh view. That can be big stuff.

Next, what are the focus areas in career? There's space for four in the layout, but of course you define what's reasonable for you. You might have already discovered that you want to downsize in the career department and call it a job. Or you may have discovered that you have had a series of jobs and you now want a career. Whatever you have learned, use it to define the areas of focus for you.

Again, the areas of focus have to align with and support the whole life strategy. Creatively marketing cigarettes to young adults doesn't line up well with a focus on (passion for) health and fitness (sorry, it just doesn't.) But if you have a passion for caring for the environment, you could have a career focus element on sustainable packaging, or reducing workplace waste, or donating a percentage of profits to a cause you support.

Hey, here's an idea: using what you learned from Steps 3: Curiosity, 4: Challenge and 5: Choose, you might be able to add in areas of focus in your career that align more closely with your life strategy *and* help you see opportunities for fulfillment, growth, satisfaction and movement that you hadn't seen before. They could be small or big. They might start out small and open big doors. Perspective again.

Last step, write your vision statement for your career. All the same stuff applies. It's for you; it needs to reflect your dream, and you gotta love it. Don't be sidetracked by trying to figure out how you'll get it. Don't get pulled down by the context of your current crisis. It's your dream. When you've crafted it, it goes next to the life vision. Just do a safety check and make sure you've worded it in a way that aligns with the way you've worded your life vision. Words matter, remember.

And you now have your completed career strategy document integrated as part of your whole life strategy. Notice "what you have to do" is **not** part of your career strategy. So getting a new job, changing careers, upgrading your skills…those are not part of your strategy. Those will be actions that you take to achieve your strategy. We'll talk about that a bit in the coming chapter. But I'm not gonna tell you what job you should have, or what career you should go into…that's your choice, and you've been working on that particular superpower. Besides, there are lots of good books and tools out there to help you figure that out. It'll be a lot easier now that you've played with your options and you have built a strategy, because you have your strategy for navigational guidance, and you can use it to spot check the direction of your ideas, to see if they fit. You've also planted quite a few seeds to get your brain started on solving problems.

• • •

So this whole chapter is one big exercise about alignment and integration. Aren't you impressed by how well it integrates making it real, making it yours and doing an exercise?

Download the workbook here www.OhSnap-theBook.com/

JOT SPOT

Oh, did I catch you without some sticky notes??
Jot a quick note here, you can expand later in the workbook!

Part III

POST-STRATEGY

"How come the Muggles don't hear the bus?" said Harry.

"Them!" said Stan contemptuously. "Don' listen properly, do they? Don' look properly either. Never notice nuffink, they don'."

—**J.K. Rowling**, *Harry Potter and the Prisoner of Azkaban*

Okay, now you have your strategy. What happens next? What does that mean? What do I do? Am I finished? Will things just magically change for me now?

It depends, let me explain, you'll see, no, yes and no. There, does that help? I know, I'm just being flippant. I apologize. I'm sure you have serious questions about what comes next, and I will answer them as seriously—and helpfully—as I can.

Here's what's coming up. In Chapter 9, Execution is all about executing your strategy, not walking up to the guillotine.

In Chapter 10, I'll talk a bit about some of the specifics around culture, values and interviewing your opportunities to see if they fit you—a bit of a flip from how we usually think about interviews. In Chapter 11, I'll talk about the leftover questions, the "what-ifs".

But I do want to take a moment here to answer the last two questions above.

Are you finished? Nope, no way. You aren't finished until you are finished. I mentioned before that your strategy is a living thing, and that will be true as long as you are a living thing. You might make minor adjustments along the way as you move through your life. Or you might want big changes, as you move into a different phase of your life, complete experiences or discover brand new opportunities. The point is, that's all okay, as long as you are aware and Choose (use the super power). You don't want to find that you accidentally got somewhere you didn't really want to be, right? A little spontaneity and accidental adventure is freakin' awesome, but too much means you aren't really in control of your life experience.

Will things just magically change for me now? This is the biggie, and the answer is yes and no. Things will change, and it will seem to be by magic. All the synchronicity stuff (apologies for the technical jargon) and clarity, focus, awareness and attraction—that can feel like magic. The power of intention can really feel like magic! You'll be manifesting your own destiny with mysterious super powers. I explained a little of how it works in your brain, but if you want to feel like it is magic because it makes you happier, that is totally fine. Magic is special, right? Magic seems like a lot less work than forcing things to go the way you want them. (It is!) That's also why superpowers are so great. You have them as long as you use them for good. So yes, you can think of it as magic, as long as you put it into a Harry Potter like context. You are still responsible for what happens, you are not the victim of fate. You are not a muggle. That's really what's going on. You are more aware now—aware of what you want, of your powers and how to access them.

If you're wondering why I did this seemingly random jump into the land of muggles and magic, it's because I want you to understand how much impact having a strategy can have. It's like the point in the Wizard of Oz movie when it goes from black and white to technicolor. Having a strategy can really change the way you see the world. It can *absolutely* change how you navigate in the world! Having a guiding star means that you are never lost. That **can** change everything, if you let it.

One more thing about magic. Magic is fun. You should know that you are no longer in crisis mode, because you have decided where you want to go. Next you'll figure out how to get there. Make it fun. Fun is enjoyment, amusement or lighthearted pleasure. It's fun being completely absorbed in an experience. Find your fun and take it along into the next chapter. I guess I'm saying, "Welcome to your future. Enjoy the ride!"

. . . .
JOT SPOT
. . . .

Oh, did I catch you without some sticky notes??
Jot a quick note here, you can expand later in the workbook!

Chapter 9

EXECUTiON

• • • • • • • • • • •

"*A good plan is like a road map: it shows the final destination and usually the best way to get there.*"

—H. Stanley Judd

"*Well, duh.*"*—me, but not in response to H. Stanley Judd*

Now what?

NOW you are ready to take action. Not random action, planned action. Which means, of course, that you want to have a plan. You have a start, because you've identified your goals—they are your outcomes.

Actually, I think you really know how to do this already. Action has always been your strong suit. Once you know what to do, you know how to do it. So I apologize in advance if any of this chapter seems really boring because you already know this stuff. Feel free to skim. But just maybe I'll make a point you haven't thought of yet, or lead you to an insight. And there's always the thing about how easy it is to see things for other people, or at work, and how it's harder to see and apply to yourself. Just sayin'.

The basics: A plan is not just a series of to-do items, it's richer than that. A plan is a series of steps that you've identified to get you where you want to be, along with timing and a list of what you need to bring with you. When you build your plan, you understand that there is some sequencing that needs to go on, some dependencies. Of course, you are also making assumptions, and you'll want to call those out. Your plan is specific to your strategy. The things that you are going to identify are going to be different from anyone else, because (repeat after me) it has to align with your life strategy. You may have seen or heard or read about the expert's advice on how to do X, and while you may want to take that into consideration, it's probably not going to be a 100% fit for you. You're going to have to customize for you. You have to build your own plan.

I'm sure you have your own methodology for building a plan. Here's mine. It's totally stolen, I mean adapted, from my time leading software development and performance improvement projects. I build the plan in layers.

The first layer is building a roadmap, and it's pretty much preparation for the plan.

Step one is always an assessment: current state and future state, or "is" and "to be". Where are we now and where to do we want to be? You've done most of that already, in the clarity work. I lay out the goals (outcomes) in a high level roadmap, so that I have a visual perspective of the journey. Hey, you have the major bits in your strategy! How handy!

Step two is an analysis: what are the gaps between current and future states? What needs to happen to be able to get there from here? Not the how, just the what. You haven't done exactly this yet, but I bet you've started thinking about it. The "what needs to happen" are your major milestones. When you write them out, remember that words matter. So write them as if they have already been achieved. Here's an example: think about the difference in the wording between "take the bar exam", "pass the bar exam" and "bar exam passed". "Take" feels a bit overwhelming and doesn't even include the bit about needing to pass, "pass" feels better, but "bar exam passed" feels best of all, because it expresses the goal being accomplished. In this prep work, stay high level. No point getting distracted or discouraged trying to figure out details!

You know what I'm going to say here, right? You can use stickies for this! I recommend that you have several colors available, and that you use a different one for your outcomes and for milestones.

Okay, now it's time to flesh out the plan.

Start with your roadmap (in the workbook), which has your outcomes laid out on a timeline. Make sure your timeline actually has time on it! How long are you allowing between each outcome? Create intervals that make sense between each outcome. It might make sense to have short intervals for your short term outcome (weekly or monthly) but that would make no sense to have between your mid and long term outcomes, because your plan just isn't going to be that granular!

Next, place out the major milestones between the goals, sequenced along your timeline. There, that's done. Seriously, you have a more detailed roadmap, and that's all you need for the longer term stuff.

You do want a detailed plan for the shorter term, though. Why not for the long term? It would be a waste of time. Too much will change between now and then. You will probably find a short cut. You will absolutely discover a lot more information that will be relevant. So you're finding a good balance between preparation and just-in-time. Some things have long lead-times, some have short ones. Finding the sweet spot gives you a lot of flexibility to seize opportunities when they show up, and still have the resources you need to get things done. You're not ignoring the future, but you're not obsessing on it either. You are doing what you can do now—that's what sequencing the milestones is all about. If you think you need to plant a few more milestones now, go ahead! It's just stickies, right? Sure, you aren't going to leave them on your wall forever. You want to document your roadmap.

For the short term, you're going to need a bigger wall, because you're going to add a lot more detail. You want to identify the steps to achieve the milestones. Yes, that is the how. You also want to think through the resources you'll need in each step. Resources are usually time, money and people, but they can also be expertise, physical resources, etc. Some of your steps might be lining up the resources!

And of course, you want to call out any assumptions you make. Here's a hint: you can use the approach from Step 4 where you call out your assumptions, challenge them and look for creative ways to resolve any issues. Emphasis on creative. Is there another way to get what you need? Can you make it fun? Can you combine things? Can someone help you? Can you pull in transferrable skills? Can you find a way to do it for free? Can you combine it with something you are passionate about? How can it fit well into your life and your other priorities?

Another way to look creatively at your plan is to work backwards. Start at your outcome or milestone and say "what needs to happen right before this?" and keep going in that direction. That can help you be thorough, but it can also help you get rid of things that aren't really necessary. It's a different way of sequencing that can break through blocks.

And speaking of blocks…what if you just don't know exactly how to get where you want to go? What if you don't know all of the steps? Or what if this whole planning thing is just too hard and it makes your head hurt. The truly fantastic news is that you really don't have to know all of that now. You have your roadmap. You can start with that, because you have clarity on what you want and your strategy. That gives you awareness, synchronicity and access to your superpowers—the magic stuff, right? There's one more little bonus that comes with it, too—inspired action.

You don't need to know every detail of how you are going to achieve your goals. You really only need to know the next few steps—and that's what inspired action is. If it's dark outside, you don't need for it to be day. You don't need to light up the whole forest. You just need enough lighting for a few steps on the path, the part that is right in front of you. Inspired action is like having little flashlights on your feet, so the next few steps are always lit up. It takes a lot less energy for a flashlight than a bunch of floodlights.

The flashlights come from the work you've done on clarity. You know what you want. You check in on each step to make sure that it is going to get you closer to what you want and that it aligns with your strategy. You check in with your values and priorities. Does it fit? Okay. If you aren't sure about something, ask yourself "what would the future me do? The one who has already achieved the outcome?" Don't ask what someone else would do—even if they are totally awesome—because they aren't you, and you are looking for the answer that fits you and your life.

The flashlights on your feet help you keep focus on what is right in front of you. They help you to focus on the actions you need to take right now. They can keep you from wasting your time on things that are not on your path, that have nothing to do with getting you further down your path. You know, like sending out resumes and interviewing for things that really aren't what you want, and won't get you there. Or maybe even like putting in ridiculous hours at your current job doing things that don't get you any further down your path. Or getting all caught up in work politics and ambitions that don't align with your values and priorities.

The flashlights on your feet can also light up the immediate opportunities that you wouldn't have otherwise seen.

Once you get started down the path, remember to check your compass periodically—your strategy, your north star—to make sure that you're still headed in the right direction. Keep track of your progress. Celebrate your progress! That's how you live into your strategy.

Making It Yours

Now you can do the job change thing, or the career change thing, or not—whatever is on *your* plan. Your plan isn't filled with a bunch of activities that might get you near your goal, and it's definitely not a scattershot approach. Focus your attention and energy on the activities on your plan. If for some reason they don't seem to be working, you can adjust your plan and your path, a few steps at a time, but keeping your ultimate outcomes in mind. Look for more inspired actions. Is there a different way to get to your outcome? It's a good thing that you don't have to revise a whole project plan, right? Just make some adjustments, based on what you learned!

If you identify a pretty major step, one that you think might be a bit challenging for you, or has an impact on other people, you might want to use some change management skills. That's definitely a transferrable set of skills from the world of business. When smart companies want to be successful in transforming something—whether it's implementing a new software program or a reorganization or acquisition or whatever—they invest in change management. It's a strong discipline, and we can apply the principles to our personal lives to be more successful. You can read more about this in my book, *Whoops! I Forgot to Achieve My Potential.* Some of the key principles are: communicate what's going on to people who are impacted, involve people in the change, identify potential risks and come up with ways to mitigate them, learn from successes and failures, and celebrate successes along the way! I highly recommend creating a personal change management strategy!

Exercise: Graphical Roadmap

In the workbook, there is a graphical template for your roadmap. It's smaller, so it'll be a lot easier to fold than a real roadmap, but it can still be pretty handy to pull out for those periodic check-ins.

· · · · · · · · ·
JOT SPOT
· · · · · · · · ·

Oh, did I catch you without some sticky notes??
Jot a quick note here, you can expand later in the workbook!

Chapter 10

CULTURE, VALUES AND OTHER RANDOM STUFF

● ●

"Our number one priority is company culture. Our whole belief is that if you get the culture right, most of the other stuff, like delivering great customer service or building a long-term enduring brand will just happen naturally on its own."

"The conditions of the training encourage people to take a real look at what Zappos is like and to think about a thing like happiness in the larger picture of their overall employment. It encourages people to go home, talk to their friends and family and ask themselves "Is this a company I really believe in? Is this a culture I really want to be a part of and contribute to?"

—**Tony Hsieh**, CEO, Zappos (pre-Amazon days)

Really quickly, I just want to make a couple of points. I wouldn't normally have to say this stuff, but you've recently been in a crisis. You might be a bit beaten down. Most of my clients are, and it's not really their fault, but they do need to snap out of it. It's my hope that by the time you get to this point in the book that you are no longer in crisis mode, whether it's because you've changed your perspective or whether you've taken action to change your circumstances. No matter what, though, there's a decent chance that you currently are or will soon be looking for some kind of job change. I want to remind you that you are a good human being with a lot to offer, because frankly, the process for changing jobs can be a bit demoralizing. The decisions can be difficult. I want you to make your choices using your superpower, not from a feeling of worthlessness or powerlessness.

You might have discovered as you were drafting your strategy that there is a conflict between your current company and your personal values. You may have known that it was there, but admitting that you really aren't two people and you only have one set of values might have brought the conflict to the forefront. That may mean you need to make a change to a different company that aligns better with you. Don't underestimate the importance of culture and values—a misalignment could have been a big contributing factor to your crisis. A mismatch of culture or values is actually a great reason to leave, especially if you can do it before you compromise yourself, make yourself miserable, or worse, become immune.

If there is a mismatch, you may be tempted to stay and try to change it. You might even feel obligated to try. If so, ask yourself these questions: Can you actually change the culture? Do you have enough influence? How deeply embedded is the culture? Do you want to stay and try to change it? Is it your job to change it? Would it take too much out of you, or would you feel great satisfaction trying to make the change?

You may choose to make a change for other reasons, too. If it ends up that a job, company or career change is in your future, you are going to go on interviews and you will have to make choices. When you go on an interview, remember that you have as much right to interview them as they do to interview you. You are looking for a match. You are not at anyone's mercy, you have choices, and they are lucky to have you as a candidate. There could be a whole bunch of "nos" out there waiting for you. Awesome, wow. It's kinda like dating. You can be sad if you're rejected, but if they aren't the one, don't you want to know sooner rather than later? It's also true that many of the initial interview stages are designed to screen people out, not to actually hire people, so don't take it personally! Do your research and see if they are a match for you, too. You both get a say in the matter.

The interviewer might be looking at your skills, resume and experience to see if you are a match, but they are also looking at your personality and values to see if you are a fit for the culture. You should be doing the same, right from the beginning. Culture is hugely important in determining whether the two of you are a match. So check it out.

Research the company ahead of time. You can research the company online and in the community. You can check out the company website, and often find clues by poking around, reading the annual report and press releases. You can investigate on Glassdoor.com, but remember that disgruntled people are motivated to post, so take posts with a grain of salt. See if you know anyone who works for the company, partners with the company, is a vendor or customer, etc. LinkedIn is great for this. Ask them questions about culture.

Arrive early and look around. What's on the walls? How are visitors treated. Observe some employee interactions. Look at their facial expressions, body language, dress, etc. Does it feel comfortable to you? Can you see yourself there?

Take time during the interview to ask questions to find out as much as you can about the culture and values.

You can also get a little more information by asking questions during the interview process. Obvious things are to ask about vision and value statements, policies on diversity, development. Ask about the review process, what kind of behavior is encouraged, rewarded and how. Ask how the company handles performance issues. Ask about things that matter to you, such as dress code, flexible work schedule, working from home, sponsored education, diversity in hiring, promoting from within, cross-functional opportunities, improvement projects, investment in infrastructure, overtime, working weekends, work/life balance policies—whatever matters to you. Ask how information flows through the company, poke for transparency or secrecy. Ask what the most controversial policies have been, and why.

Follow up by asking to walk through the workplace and talk to an employee or two. Ask them similar questions, and see if the answers are the same. That will tell you how much is policy and management speak or really part of the culture. While you're at it, ask about the department you'd be working in and your potential boss. Pay attention to your gut responses and to the overall vibe.

Of course you don't want this to seem like an inquisition, so be curious and conversational. Don't come across as judgmental, or you won't get real answers.

One more thing. Don't work for a jerk. No matter what. Life is too short. Spend time finding out about your potential boss or leadership team. Ask to talk to some other people on the team.

You can ask them what it's like to work for your potential boss. They may not be completely open, but you can probably read between the lines.

Okay, one more thing. Say you do take a new job, and within a short period of time you discover that it was a mistake. Fix it quickly. Don't stay for the requisite year so that it looks good on your resume, or so that you don't have to explain a difficult situation. You'll just end up in a crisis again in a very short time. So take corrective action as soon as you can, following your north star. Don't let the experience beat you down so that you distrust yourself. Identify the lessons and learn from the experience so that you don't repeat it. Be grateful that you caught on early.

Oh, I forgot, there's just one more thing. You might decide to stay where you are. You may have discovered that you actually like your job, and it supports your life strategy. You were just listening to other people's thoughts so much that you thought you should be in a crisis. But you aren't. Woo hoo!

Okay that's it. You've got this.

• • • • • • • •
JOT SPOT
• • • • • • • •

Oh, did I catch you without some sticky notes??
Jot a quick note here, you can expand later in the workbook!

Chapter 11

NOW WHAT IF?

• • • • • • • • • • • • • • • •

"Good morning. You are perfectly cast in your life. I can't imagine anyone but you in the role. Go play."
—tweet from **Lin-Manuel Miranda** 4/29/2016

O kay, here you are. The last chapter. Maybe you've read through the book once and are going to go back and do all the exercises and create your strategy. Fantastic, that is a great way to do it. Perhaps you worked your way through, doing the exercises as you went along. Fantastic, that's also a great way to do it. In either case, you may want to come back here in a while and check in.

I want to answer some questions you might have.

What if… you've done all the work, made some career changes and discovered that the problem really isn't your job? That's not at all unusual! Work and career are often the symptom, not the cause.

So how do you "fix" your life? The solution is probably not to just go find another job. Go back to your web of life assessment. Take it again, if things have changed. Look at the areas where there are the biggest gaps. Look back at the work you did to identify ways to add in things that help address the gaps. Then do it—add them in! You can build—and execute—a plan to get to the outcomes you identified for your life strategy. That's probably an obvious answer. But if you're stuck, check out my first book, *Whoops! I Forgot to Achieve My Potential.* Follow this link for a free pdf www. OhSnap-theBook.com/. If you want a paperback copy, you can get it on Amazon http://amzn.to/29SWoIW.

What if… you did the work, you have a strategy, you made the changes, but you find yourself back where you started. You're back in a crisis. You feel the same. No matter what you do, you end up in the same place. It's kind of like the movie Groundhog Day. You probably have some outdated beliefs that are holding you back. Check out *WTF?!? I Still Believe This Sh*t?* Follow this link for a free pdf. www.OhSnap-theBook.com/ If you want a paperback copy, you can get it on Amazon, too http://amzn.to/29YSdir.

What if…you have the best intentions, but you can't keep the momentum going. You slide right back into old habits and before you know it, a month has gone by and you haven't actually done anything—except maybe you notice you are complaining a lot again! You need accountability and support, my friend. You might be able to get that from a friend who is going through the same thing—an accountability partner. You might find a group to join. You would probably do really, really well with a life coach.

What if…the fix is really longer term, and it will take you a while to get where you want to be. The reality is that there are bills to pay. It is okay—totally okay—to just "get a job" as a stop-gap measure, as long as you are aware that's what you're doing. Don't fool yourself. Keep that in mind and keep working on the longer terms goals. Don't settle. Be conscious of the fact that this is a stepping stone job that is enabling you to get further along on your path. No, you don't have to tell your employer that! Just be a good employee and give them their money's worth.

On a sort of related note...our identity is really wrapped up in our work. I've found it to be especially true for men who are subject to a set of huge social pressures. When we are out of work, we have a hard time because we aren't completely sure who we are. I think there's also some social pressure that tells us that if we aren't working, we aren't sure of our value. Sad, but reality. Think about it. When you meet people for the first time, how often do they ask "what do you do?" How many people check in with you by asking "how's work?" How often do you introduce yourself by saying your name and your profession? See, it's a big piece of our social identity. So, of course, we struggle when we aren't clear about that facet of our identity or when we are out of work, when "I'm an X" can't just roll smoothly off of our tongue. Be patient and kind to yourself.

And while we're on the subject of patience, you didn't get into this crisis overnight. It was the process of a long time of things getting out of whack. So be patient if it takes a while to make the changes you want to make. Enjoy the journey. Have fun. Pay extra attention to the other areas of your life, besides career. Add stuff in.

What if...you want the quick and easy way? Email me Maggie@talktomaggie.com to set up a strategy session. Work with me. I'll give you accountability, insight and support. Together we will craft your life and career strategies, figure out your immediate plan of action and get you making progress—out of crisis and into inspired action.

• • • • • • • • •
JOT SPOT
• • • • • • • • •

Oh, did I catch you without some sticky notes??
Jot a quick note here, you can expand later in the workbook!

Chapter 12

MY WISH FOR YOU

• • • • • • • • • • • • • • • • • •

Dear wonderful, glittery and glowing reader—
I have to confess a couple of things. First, I wrote this book out of order. It's part of a trilogy. I think it's supposed to be the second book, but it came out third. I think that I had a few things to get over before I could really write it. The first thing I had to get over was myself. For some reason, I didn't think writing a book about a career crisis was *important* enough. Isn't that ironic? By now you've read the introduction and all the reasons I say that a career crisis *is* important—and I stand by every single solitary word. I guess I just needed to get to the same place you were, one more time, so that I could remember just how important it truly is, and be able to speak to you about it from a real place, instead of some lofty ivory tower lecture-y kind of place.

I'm pretty sure I had to obsess on the soundtrack of *Hamilton* (the musical) before I could write this book. I have absolutely no idea how that makes a direct contribution. Well, maybe I do. I'm sure you've heard all kinds of variations on the "there is nothing new on earth" theme. Maybe you've also heard of imposter syndrome— or fraud factor. Of course you have—all of my clients have been infected to one degree or another. So have I. I think I was big-time afraid of being a fraud on the topic of career. There is so much stuff out there in the world on the topic. And I'm a life coach, not a career counselor! I don't have a brand new invention that's going to turn the career world upside down. Then comes *Hamilton*. It's a raging torrent of creativity. Yet it tells an old story with a new perspective. It puts unlikely things together in an amazing fusion of hip-hop, rap, jazz and broadway. Because of all that, it reaches people on a completely different level, and that's what I had to see. Now I am not comparing myself to Lin-Manuel Miranda. I'm just saying that I learned a lot from him about fusion and perspective as viable tools for delivering a message, and recognized those tendencies in me (in a contemporary choral acapella kind of way). It's not about invention, it's about context and translation and tools.

I had to answer the front door of my office, and even though I thought the sign clearly said "Life Coach", there was actually something about career on it. I had to get over the fact that almost all of my clients come to me, initially, with some kind of question or issue that has to do with career: Is it too late for me? What do I want to do with the rest of my life? Should I quit my job? How will I be remembered? What's my purpose? Can I have meaningful work? What do I want to be when I grow up? How do I find a career that will make me happy AND make a difference? How do I stop being a workaholic? And many more iterations. That's the front door. I needed to accept the fact that my clients came to me through that front door. It makes sense. But many leave out a different door. That sounds kinda weird. It just means that they thought that their career or their job was the biggest thing they wanted to deal with, but it turns out that they really wanted their whole life back. We do it all.

Actually, *you* do it all. I can give you guidance, show you the process, ask you life changing questions, hand you awesome tools, help you discover amazing insights, and help hold you accountable. But you have to do the work. You have to face your fears, hug your hopes, think new thoughts and start taking the steps towards the future you want. You have to tell yourself the truth. You have to stop judging yourself for your past mistakes. You gotta change. And you have to want it. Yes, yes, yes, it is MUCH easier with a coach. But I can't do it for you. That was something I needed to get over, too. I had a couple of clients, where I think I wanted it more than they wanted it. It broke my heart. I thought that maybe I didn't have the right to keep on. But then I got what I needed—a couple of signs—grateful messages from clients that told me that I helped them change their lives; more clients coming in through the career front door; inspiration for this book and an amazing response to the blogs that started it. And most of all, I have a mentor who never gave up on me, who saw what I didn't see yet, and patiently kept teaching me as if I did. I had to get over my selfishness and ego and get back to serving the people I can serve, the best way I can and however they frickin' ask for it. Right? Thank you, Angela.

Well that all sounds like a confessional, and it kind of is, but it helps explain this next part: what I wish for you.

First of all, my wish is that we get you out of crisis mode and we get you some relief, and that it only gets better from here on in. I want you to know that having a strategy will help you solve your crisis in a much more effective way than jumping straight to action. I want you to feel that you are worth the time and energy it takes.

I want you to be able to do the work, make the changes, face your fears, hug your hopes, think new thoughts and start taking the steps towards the future you want. I want you to know your truth.

I so want you to stop judging yourself for your past mistakes. I want you to really know that when you think the best of yourself, you *are* the best of yourself. That's when you play big, when you make a difference, live your best life as your highest self.

I wish for you a wonderful mentor and coach, because OH MY GOD it makes such a difference! I don't care if it's a life coach, a softball coach, a chess mentor or an awesome boss. I hope you get the experience of having a wonderful coach and mentor, *and* that you learn to give back and be a mentor for someone else when the time is right.

Mostly, I want this career crisis thing to be one of the best things that ever happens to you, because you grab it by the horns and use it as the opportunity it really is! You came in the career door, but you now know that your career is just one part of who you are. I want you to get really clear on what you want out of your precious life, what you want to do and be. I want you to craft a strategy, make decisions, take actions and change your life—for the better. I want you to find the right balance for all things that make up your life, and to be the one who is in charge.

Love, love, love,

Maggie

THE END
Hah! The beginning!

• • • • • • • • •
JOT SPOT
• • • • • • • • •

Oh, did I catch you without some sticky notes??
Jot a quick note here, you can expand later in the workbook!

THANK YOU

• • • • • • • • • • •

Thank you for reading this book and spending time with me. I hope you liked it, and I really hope it helps you get out of crisis.

To get the most out of this book, please go to the special reader's page to download the companion workbook and pdf copies of my two previous books.

I like to give people presents. It's probably a syndrome or a pathology or something. When we were kids, my sister used to make things out of tissue for us. Then she'd wrap them in tissue. It was so sweet, but we had a hard time telling the wrapping from the gift. So I'm not gonna wrap these presents, okay? I'll just tell you what they are:

- the companion workbook
- a free 50-minute strategy session
- a pdf of either of my previous two books

What if...you want the quick and easy way? Email me Maggie@talktomaggie.com to set up a strategy session. Work with me. I'll give you accountability, insight and support. Together we will craft your life and career strategies, figure out your immediate plan of action and get you making progress—out of crisis and into inspired action.

ACKNOWLEDGEMENTS

• •

Writing a book is not a solo venture. It's a well-orchestrated and rehearsed ensemble performance. When everyone knows and plays their part, the author gets to look really good, and the whole thing flows like music. That's how writing this book was for me. I'm so grateful. If I pull back the curtain, there is a whole orchestra back there—and I really want to give them a bow and a standing ovation!

My clients are my inspiration. Thank you to all of my clients who show up every time, wanting to do all the work—the fun, the fascinating, the tedious and even the difficult work. Thank you for reminding me over and over again that there is such a thing as magic! Welcome and thank you to my future clients, too, because the magic will continue.

Cynthia Kane, my developmental editor, you were an absolute dream! Writing this book was so pleasurable, thanks to you. I almost feel guilty because the process was so painless. But you didn't just make it easy, your input made the book so much better.

Angela, thank you for the Plume, your mentorship, and for matter-of-factly holding the space for me to start to answer the front door—calmly, without drama. As if I always answered that door when people knocked. All people, who are just people.

Allan, Sanford, Tim, Beth, Brian and David—the conductors—I'm a much better person and writer because I'm a singer, challenged to be prepared, listen, blend, and bring more and more care to each note.

Traci Snyder, I am so happy I found you in time for this book and the launch. You really helped me to keep all the right balances, and to remember the important things.

As always, to everyone at the Difference Press: you are amazing! Thank you, thank you, thank you!

Katie, Danny, Madison, Katlyn, Charlie, Jordan, Tabitha, Nic, Puppy and Bimfee…snapchat emojifest of love.

Thank you, launch team, for making this a really fun book launch!

Oh no…they've started the music…to everyone else I didn't get to mention…THANK YOU!!!!

ABOUT THE AUTHOR

Maggie Huffman is a life coach, speaker and the author of the bestselling books, **Whoops! I Forgot to Achieve My Potential and WTF?!? I Still Believe this Sh*t?**

Maggie spent 20 (mumble) years in the corporate world. Granted, it was in wine, but it wasn't all sipping and spitting! She led many large projects and cross-functional teams—many of them global. She had a unique career path, fixing a lot of broken systems, structures and processes, which gave her access to a wealth of tools and metaphors.

In her coaching practice today, she will use anything at all that helps her clients to take inspired action and fulfill their true and full potential. These things can come from the world of science (neuroscience, quantum physics, nutrition), from the land of corporate (project and change management, executive coaching, process improvement), the world of woo (visualizations, thought work, metaphysics), pop culture or just random fun things (humor, jargon, sticky notes and Tombow markers.)

Maggie lives in a quirky, almost imaginary world that looks suspiciously like Stars Hollow (of *Gilmore Girls* fame), with a workspace straight from the set of *The Good Witch*, except that it is in Sonoma, California, where there really isn't any snow. She thinks in a weird combination of metaphors, song lyrics and Excel.

Contact: Maggie@TalktoMaggie.com
Website: www.talktomaggie.com
Twitter: @mago727

A free eBook edition is available with the purchase of this book.

To claim your free eBook edition:

1. Download the Shelfie app.
2. Write your name in upper case in the box.
3. Use the Shelfie app to submit a photo.
4. Download your eBook to any device.

Shelfie

A free eBook edition is available
with the purchase of this print book.

CLEARLY PRINT YOUR NAME ABOVE IN UPPER CASE

Instructions to claim your free eBook edition:
1. Download the Shelfie app for Android or iOS
2. Write your name in **UPPER CASE** above
3. Use the Shelfie app to submit a photo
4. Download your eBook to any device

Print & Digital Together Forever.

Snap a photo

Free eBook

Read anywhere

www.TheMorganJamesSpeakersGroup.com

We connect Morgan James published authors with live and online events and audiences whom will benefit from their expertise.

Morgan James
Speakers Group

Morgan James makes all of our titles available
through the Library for All Charity Organizations.

www.LibraryForAll.org

3 9384 00122 5849   10/18

CPSIA information can be obtained
at www.ICGtesting.com
Printed in the USA
LVOW03s1928280717
542834LV00001B/13/P

9 781683 503439